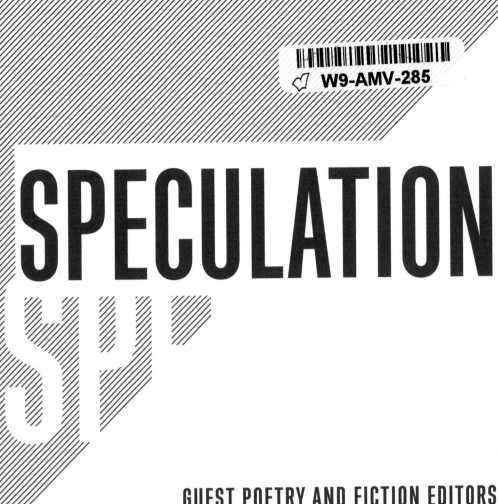

SPECULATION

GUEST POETRY AND FICTION EDITORS
ED PAVLIĆ AND IVELISSE RODRIGUEZ

Editors-in-Chief Deborah Chasman & Joshua Cohen

Senior Editor Matt Lord

Digital Director Rosie Gillies

Audience Engagement Editor Ben Schacht

Manuscript and Production Editor Hannah Liberman

Assistant to the Publishers Irina Costache

Fellowship Coordinator Jasmine Parmley

Contributing Editors Adom Getachew, Lily Hu, Walter Johnson, Robin D. G. Kelley, Paul Pierson, & Becca Rothfeld

Contributing Arts Editors Ed Pavlić & Ivelisse Rodriguez

2022 Annual Poetry Contest Judge Donika Kelly

2022 Aura Estrada Short Story Contest Judge Jordy Rosenberg

Black Voices in the Public Sphere Fellows Maya Jenkins & N'Kosi Oates

Editorial Assistants Cameron Avery & Zara Kulatunga

Finance Manager Anthony DeMusis III

Printer Sheridan PA

Board of Advisors Derek Schrier (Chair), Archon Fung, Deborah Fung, Richard M. Locke, Jeff Mayersohn, Scott Nielsen, Robert Pollin, Rob Reich, Hiram Samel, Kim Malone Scott, & Brandon M. Terry

Interior Graphic Design Zak Jensen & Alex Camlin

Cover Design Alex Camlin

Printed and bound in the United States.

Speculation is *Boston Review* issue 2023.1 (Forum 25 / 48.1 under former designation system)

A version of "Another Future Is Possible" will appear in a forthcoming anthology entitled *Finance Aesthetics: A Critical Glossary.* Thank you to the editors of that project for granting permission to publish this contribution. The anthology is due to be published with Goldsmiths University Press next year (Tygstrup et al., 2024).

"Cassandra Data" is excerpted from a longer work by Sandra Simonds.

To become a member, visit
bostonreview.net/membership/

For questions about donations and major gifts,
contact Rosie Gillies, rosie@bostonreview.net

For questions about memberships, email
members@bostonreview.net

Boston Review
PO Box 390568
Cambridge, MA 02139

ISSN: 0734-2306 / ISBN: 978-1-946511-76-8

CONTENTS

Editors' Note   6
DEBORAH CHASMAN & HANNAH LIBERMAN

Another Future Is Possible   8
ARIS KOMPOROZOS-ATHANASIOU

The Origin of Cow Therapy   18
PARASHAR KULKARNI

Two Poems   34
NJOKU NONSO

Unleashing Nightmares: Octavia Butler's Heart of Darkness
JUNOT DÍAZ   37

Two Poems   46
ABU BAKR SADIQ

Exodus   50
AMANDA RIZKALLA

Saint Lillie   71
ALEXIS V. JACKSON

The New Moral Mathematics   74
KIERAN SETIYA

Cassandra Data   92
SANDRA SIMONDS

The God Gene   94
CHRISTINA DRILL

Footage of Benjamin, the Last Living Tasmanian
Tiger—1935, Colorized   103
KRISTIN EMANUEL

It's a Thing   106
KENDA MUTONGI

Cat of Nine Tails   112
KELLY MCCORKENDALE

Two Poems   138
ASHLEY WARNER

An Island Without Sea   141
SWATI PRASAD

Little Rock Squawk or Perseverance at the Pond   158
EVARISTO RIVERA

Post-Literature   162
IAN MAXTON

Angels of History   179
ANDY BATTLE

CONTRIBUTORS   189

EDITORS' NOTE
Deborah Chasman & Hannah Liberman

ART CAN POSSESS the prophetic quality to imagine where we are going. It is perhaps no surprise, then, that in a world-historical moment of global upheaval and transformation, speculative writing is enjoying a renaissance. As a creative faculty, speculation is Janus-faced, looking to the past as well as the future.

The word itself has two opposed senses. On the one hand, speculation about land and resources has fueled colonialism and empire, the booms and busts of commodities markets, and the ecological extraction that has put our planet on a path of climate devastation. But speculation also has a constructive meaning: it can help us plot new paths to a more just world. When we speculate, we take a risk, daring to reject dominant ideas about what is possible. As sociologist Aris Komporozos-Athanasiou puts it in his contribution, "speculation tosses the coin of uncertainty in the hope of seeing through a haze-draped future." It in this sense that some of the most influential social movements today might be said to be radically speculative: Black

Lives Matter envisions a world free of racial violence, just as #MeToo imagines a world free of gendered violence.

The texts in this volume—poetry, stories, and essays—approach speculation in multiple ways. Creative works range over violence and healing, memory and erasure, and alternative worlds. Kenda Mutongi reflects on the meaning of land and community in the African diaspora. Junot Díaz celebrates the speculative fiction of Octavia Butler. Kieran Setiya investigates the ethics of the far future. Taken together, they suggest that speculation is ultimately about "our relationships with one another," as Andy Battle concludes: "what they have been, what they are, and most important, *what they could be.*"

We thank former *Boston Review* arts editor Adam McGee, contributing poetry editor Ed Pavlić, and contributing fiction editor Ivelisse Rodriguez for all their help realizing this issue. We're also grateful to our 2022 poetry and fiction contest judges, Donika Kelly and Jordy Rosenberg.

ANOTHER FUTURE IS POSSIBLE
Aris Komporozos-Athanasiou

The cautious merchant and the keen manufacturer were equally unable to resist the speculation. It spread among them like a leprosy. It ruined alike the innocent and the guilty. It periled many a humble home; it agitated many a princely dwelling. Men hastened to be rich and they were ruined. They bought largely; they subscribed eagerly; they forsook their counting-houses or companies; if successful they continued on their course, and if the reverse they too often added to the misery of the homes they had already desolated, by destroying themselves.

—John Francis on the 1846 Railway Mania

The only thing that makes life possible is permanent, intolerable uncertainty: not knowing what comes next.

—Ursula K. Le Guin

WHETHER IN MARKETS or in philosophy, speculation tosses the coin of uncertainty in the hope of seeing through a haze-draped future. A mirror (*speculum*) and a watchtower (*specula*), it animates a certain vision. From the leaps of scientific revolutions and technological futures to the pursuit of dreams and mystical theologies, speculators have always sought to capture what lies ahead.

Speculation encompasses a duality at the core of all financial activity. When pushed to its outermost limit, it can unleash formidable destructive forces and lead to the burst of market bubbles, such as seventeenth-century Amsterdam's notorious tulip craze, the Victorian era's railway manias, last century's Great Depression, or the more recent 2008 global financial crisis. During these periods, market "passions" take hold: traders venerate ethereal values with no material referents or links to "fundamentals." Yet speculation is also the market's indispensable lubricant. All speculative trades calibrate risks to generate yields and prevent markets from "overheating." Here's the definition of "speculation" provided by the *Oxford Dictionary of Finance and Banking*:

> The purchase or sale of something for the sole purpose of making a capital gain. For professional speculators the security, commodity, and foreign exchange markets are natural venues as they cater for speculation as well as investment and trading. Indeed, speculators help to make a viable market and thus smooth out price fluctuations. This is particularly true of commodity futures and option markets.

Speculation's greatest gift to markets is stability, not crisis: absorbing volatility by "smooth[ing] out price fluctuations" and generating liquidity. For those in the business of trading, speculation means betting on possible future movements of asset prices, but it also involves dealing in risky assets (including derivatives and futures) with the goal of providing insurance *against* price movements. Speculators, in other words, both "short" and "hedge" uncertainty. Throughout capitalism's history, defenders and opponents of speculation have foregrounded one function over the other to mark it as a virtue or as a vice.

ICONIC ANARCHIST thinker Pierre-Joseph Proudhon, in his 1857 *Stock Exchange Speculator's Manual*, famously distinguished between the greedy financiers of the Paris stock market—whom he lamented as "pure, corrupt, and unproductive gamblers"—and what he saw as more productive forms of speculation. When sought for its own sake, speculation is circular, autotelic, and parasitic on the real economy. When put to "productive use," however, it can also be generative, exciting, and imaginative: a source of the "the genius of discovery . . . that invents, innovates . . . [and] creates something from nothing."

As markets in the global centers of capitalism sought to expand their insatiable financial activities over the course of the nineteenth century, they vied fervently for control over the power of speculation. Just as Proudhon was writing his *Manual*, a new kind of speculative market was being established some four thousand miles west of the Paris Bourse. In 1848 the Chicago Board of Trade (CBOT) was founded. In the coming decades, it would become the world's first organized exchange for futures contracts: standardized agreements to buy or sell an "underlying asset" (predominantly grains such as wheat from the city's hinterland), at a guaranteed price for delivery at a specified future time. Trading futures ostensibly served the hedging side of speculation's coin, functioning as insurance against volatility for farmers whose harvest was exposed to radical and incalculable weather uncertainties.

Speculators stepped in to take on the unwanted risk at a discount (thus performing a social function), while farmers received security and the market remained liquid. Yet no bushels of grain were being moved because of these trades, and actual contracts never exchanged hands in the CBOT. Soon after the launch of the future contract, the circulation of "phantom wheat" in the pit vastly overtook that of the real grain produced in farms; futures traders engaged in "fictitious dealings" that were entirely unmoored from the corporeal economy. Was this kind of speculation ethical? Was it different from ordinary gambling? Advocates of futures contracts and the CBOT's influential allies believed so. State courts enshrined the legal right of futures traders to short sell for their alleged positive effect on setting off prices in the real economy, and successive governments sanctioned the promise of even the most fictitious of trades "to financially stabilize an inherently unstable capitalism." Importantly, speculative bets made in the pit were painstakingly distinguished from the wagers placed outside of incorporated commodities, which were systematically slated. In the mushrooming bucket shops (informal establishments open to anyone who wanted to wager small sums on the price movements of stocks in formal exchanges) strewing U.S. cities of the *fin de siècle*, speculation was becoming a game for the many.

This was the disorganized speculation associated typically with farmers and people of color, with migrant urban workers and women—groups that were not only excluded from the futures markets (even through, for some, these markets defined the prices of their products and hence their livelihoods) but were also derided as morally repugnant. The imagined netherworld of dingy gambling houses served as a convenient scapegoat to the celestial halls of futures trading. By transposing the evils of speculation to outcast lay bettors, the pits' denizens and their powerful institutional allies buttressed the legitimacy of *Homo economicus*. They cast it as a noble figure and stood it at the helm of U.S. capitalism.

Yet speculative activities across organized exchanges and informal bucket shops had deeper affinities in the Victorian era. Speculators from all walks of life wielded a vivid imagination to navigate the inherent opacity of staking the future. Flight from reality was not the exclusive purview of irrational and exuberant "crowds." Professional financiers, too, regularly turned to occult technologies of market prognostication, their speculations meandering through the worlds of magic, superstition, and tarot card reading. Stock markets' close encounter with astrology is perhaps the most telling of this enmeshment of the rational/scientific and the irrational/spiritual: Wall Street traders lined up to heed the predictions of financial astrologers such as the notorious Evangeline Adams, while mainstream financial technologies were adopting horoscopic methods that sought to map the movements of markets onto those of stars.

In the dawn of finance capitalism's modern era, speculation created a world that was at once obscure and spectacular, full of stardust and bitter conflicts—a world that was far from insulated from broader social reality. Speculators were a mirror image of society rather than a deviation from it, reflecting its drive to lay wagers on the unknown in the face of radical uncertainty.

THIS WORLD is one we can still recognize as ours. Following a period of unbridled financialization during the later part of the twentieth century (heralded by the momentous repeal of the Glass-Steagall legislation allowing commercial banks to act as financial traders), contemporary economies and societies are once again steeped in the whirlpool of speculation. In today's turbocharged financial markets, speculation is even more opaque because of the highly complex technologies on which it relies: machine learning, algorithmically powered, superfast trading systems whose inner workings are often indiscernible even to traders themselves. High-frequency automated trading takes place in virtual pits, with data scientists and coders quietly monitoring a ceaseless search for patterns through stacks of data, including predictive analysis of social media content that informs trading decisions (not all that different from the practices of yesteryear's financial astrologists).

On the most obscure end of these markets, speculators submerge themselves in "dark pools," which are exclusive forums for block trading securities that evade transparency requirements of formal exchanges, where dealings appear even more detached from reality. The complexity of this kind of trading means that it is often impossible to tell whether a product like the derivative will be used to hedge an uncertain event or derive profit from it. At the same time, speculative wagers are now placed not merely on the uncertainty of the future, but also on the volatility of uncertainty itself. At Chicago's CBOE, a spinoff of the CBOT and the largest modern options exchange in the United States, volatility has its own index commonly called the VIX or "fear index"—a measure of expected price swings in the S&P options market. CBOE's virtual pit even trades volatility as an "asset class" with its own "index futures."

The denizens of these new temples of finance continue to fire up the public imagination. On first blush, we may intuitively recall the greedy yet charming hedge funders—immortalized by Leonardo DiCaprio's gregarious performance as Jordan Belfort in the 2013 film *The Wolf of*

Wall Street—as the exemplary speculators of our time. But on closer inspection, a new and more tragic figure is emerging to usurp the suave megatrader of financialized capitalism from its throne. The modern-day speculator resembles Dr. Alexander Hoffmann, the tragic high-tech Frankenstein protagonist of Robert Harris's 2011 bestseller *The Fear Index*: a tormented physicist-cum-financier confronted with VIXAL-4, an omniscient AI algorithm with the power to predict fear—including Dr. Hoffmann's own fear of losing himself entirely in a battle with the mercurial forces of finance. The novel was adapted to a TV series with actor Josh Hartnett rummaging the streets of Geneva injured, haunted, limping, and sweating while searching for clues to his own past and future, plunged into a nightmare reality where it is impossible to distinguish fact from fiction.

Yet beyond this dreamlike world of hyper-technologized finance, contemporary markets' thirst for volatility is reminiscent of our own immersion in the gamified reality of financialized digital media, where speculation breaks out of the organized digital pits to become a mass spectacle. With retail trading of highly volatile assets exploding in the post-2008 crisis era, meme stocks and crypto trading platforms, decentralized finance ("defi") and decentralized applications ("dApps") provide the online bucket shops for our time's virtual punters. Mass "shorting" events such as the GameStop saga—a grassroots short squeeze on the price of the iconic video game retailer organized via social media and making headlines in January 2021—betray a world where volatility is treated as an opportunity in society writ large, with ordinary people sowing (rather than averting) uncertainty to reap profit. Following a long trail of speculators for whom the worlds of wizardry and reason were never too far apart, today's short-sellers care little about untangling reality and fiction in their "augmented" everyday lives, from the Metaverse and Web 3.0 to the in-game trading of nonfungible tokens. They are drawn to strange narratives, increasingly untethered from material reality and woven into the mainstream. Perhaps most alarmingly, the confusion sown by this radical fragmentation of everyday experiences promotes right-wing conspiracy fantasies and regressive movements such as QAnon, which are moving rapidly from the fringes of political discourse to center stage.

Under such conditions speculation once again emerges as an apt and imaginative response to the chaotic volatility wrought by financialized life—importantly, as a collective rather than merely individual act. The kind of speculation involved in these gamified worlds evokes a yearning for community and imagined connectivity, a joint "hedging" of uncertainty. Wagers across the economy and politics—from "crypto bros" coordinating their short sells around meme stocks to profit from destabilized prices to voters in Middle England sowing Brexit chaos in the hope of disrupting the liberal-technocratic status quo—are oriented toward new solidarities and often confusing political alliances. Such speculations place demands on the future in ways that encompass (rather than redress) doubt, ambivalence, and cynicism.

Speculation is a definitive feature of contemporary life across the spheres of economy and politics. Since the early stages of nineteenth-century financialized capitalism, it has often been understood as a phantasmatic or parasitic logic driving the financial markets' rapacious pursuits. But under the increasingly uncontrollable uncertainty of our financialized world, speculation also becomes a more productive mechanism to imagine community and collective coping with disorienting volatility. Speculation, in this sense, is not merely a symptom (as mainstream critiques in both economic and political theory often suggest) but a structure, something more foundational and generative. Therefore, it may also contain valuable answers to the financialization of modern life: if the only certainty about our future is its inherent indeterminacy, another future will always be possible, and fighting for it will never be futile. But how do economies and societies take up this challenge?

This proposition has implications for how we might rethink the political use of speculation. Speculation can be a weapon mobilized not only against (neo)liberal democracy (for example, in the case of nativist conspiracists and right-wing populists), but against finance itself: as an instrument for orienting a radical collective imagination toward more inclusive myths and future narratives that help those in the margins of capitalist society resist the logic of capital. As such, speculation should also be understood as a field of action that may enable movements to challenge the paradigm from which they emerge, by encouraging us to figure out who we are and who we can be in the face of radical uncertainty. How can we envision resistance in the sense of genuinely alternative life patterns, capable of defeating the oppressive forces of finance capitalism? What are forms of struggle and subjectivity that exceed the set menus of political choices offered by neoliberal risk management? How can the communities formed under the fog enveloping homo speculans nurture such alternatives? And, finally, how can the necessity of imagining the future without access to adequate resources become an instrument for overturning the conditions producing financialization in the first place?

We may call these forms of radical and progressive speculation "counter-speculation": collective political action to pursue solidarity amid uncertainty. Today we find the traces of counter-speculation when groups that are traditionally subjected to the speculative violence of finance (women, racialized, and queer people) rise to wage their own bets on the future. In doing so, they reimagine that future. As new speculative communities emerge from the allegedly invincible "There Is No Alternative" doctrine, the challenge for progressive movements will be learning to occupy this new uncharted territory of possibility. We can expose the nefarious forces of exclusionary ignorance while finding ways to retain trust in a shared reality. Better yet, we can acknowledge that such a shared reality contains the myths of our own making.

THE ORIGIN OF COW THERAPY

Parashar Kulkarni

(winner of the 2022 Boston Review *Aura Estrada Short Story Contest)*

"The Origin of Cow Therapy" is a historical novel tunneled into the dazzling space of a short story. A comedic send-up of psychiatric institutions and the self-important, ceaselessly speculating project of British hegemony, the story will have you thinking about its fully fleshed world long after you finish reading.
—Jordy Rosenberg, 2022 *Boston Review* Aura Estrada Short Story Contest judge

GAITONDE'S SECOND MONTH at the asylum began ominously. Overnight, Nandi's mud idol had transformed into a mound. No one knew who had made the idol, and it remained untouched at the corner where the residential section met the courtyard. Footprints were found but the most basic question—did they belong to an idolater or an iconoclast?—remained unanswered. Everyone knew that the act was done in the middle of the night and if the muddy spread was a sign, it was done in the throes of passion.

Administrative duties had changed. Dr. Ghose was doing the morning rounds, Dr. Mani, the evening. Still, Dr. Ghose retained his hobby. In broad daylight, he could be seen walking around with a "dirty" novel hidden in brown paper, making it appear like an innocent notebook. The miniature size, the aged papers, the crumpled edges, the end of a dry leaf sticking out from the middle, and his mischievous chuckles that pulled his upper lip down and his thin mustache up were a giveaway.

The novel couldn't survive Gaitonde's panoptic vision, and he took its illegal presence as an invitation to approach Dr. Ghose and mention to him that, despite being a patient in the asylum, he was a noted scholar who used to routinely research at the Asiatic Library.

"Where are you assigned?" Dr. Ghose asked, cutting him off.

"Nowhere yet . . . I will be happy to work in the library or in a suitable position."

"Where is this library?" the doctor smirked.

Gaitonde chewed on his nails.

At 10:00 a.m., the thin attendant in thick overalls came up to Gaitonde and asked him to join the queue meant for the inmates assigned to the occupational therapy program. Gaitonde followed the queue out of the building.

"This group, farm two, weeding," Dr. Ghose said, herding the men.

At noon, when the sun was up and burning, Gaitonde found himself in the middle of the tiny asylum farm uprooting unnamed plants and shrubs.

An hour later, when Gaitonde was famished, Ghose arrived and signaled to the attendant who ran down to Gaitonde and pulled him out.

"You will read a newspaper to a patient in the European section, an English patient. The first two pages, every other day, at nine in the morning. Do you understand? I will take you there myself. It's on the other side of the asylum. You start on Monday," Ghose said.

"PUT THIS ON," Ghose said, handing Gaitonde a coarse but clean cotton shirt and pants. Usually, all inmates wore cotton dhotis, a vest, and chappals. Gaitonde, with Dr. Ghose by his side, walked past the wrought iron gate chipped with age that connected the paying and the non-paying patients, through the work shed, and finally to a similar gate that separated the European section. He handed Gaitonde to the medical officer. The inmates called the medical officer of the European section the Clark Gable of India. He wore a trimmed flat mustache, pomade hair pressed to the right, and a linen shirt folded at the sleeves. He tried to match up but officially he was still Dr. J. Johnson, raised in Darjeeling in a devout Presbyterian family from Edinburgh.

"You must be careful. Don't annoy him. Read the paper and leave. If he says he is Churchill, say yes, but don't believe him."

They turned to the residential section and walked through a sun-bleached corridor with rooms on either side. Johnson stopped at No. 105, knocked, and stepped in. Gaitonde followed. The room was large and airy, white-washed like the corridor outside. It was an austere setup—a wooden cot with a once-blue but now discolored mosquito net, a table covered with a flower-embroidered cloth, two wooden rattan wicker armchairs, a veranda looking out to the yard, and light curtains playing

Kulkarni

with the breeze. Gaitonde stepped in. A man in an army uniform, baldish, was sitting behind the table looking out of the window toward a green yard shaded by a Gulmohar tree at the peak of its blossom. His legs were stretched onto the windowsill. He twirled a pencil. There was no paper.

"Hello long ears," the man said without turning.

"Hello young man," Johnson responded. "You asked for—"

"Want to hear a joke?" he asked.

"Yes," Gaitonde said.

"Once, I, Stalin, and Roosevelt were in a car that stopped in the middle of the road. We rolled down the window to find a huge bull standing in our path. I stepped out, walked to the bull, and asked him to move. He did not. Then Roosevelt got out, walked to the bull, and asked him to move. He did not. Finally, Stalin got out, walked to the bull, and whispered something in the bull's ear. The bull rose instantly and sprinted away. 'What did you tell him?' we asked. 'Nothing much,' Stalin responded, 'I told him that if you don't move, we will send you to a collective farm.'"

The man stood, turned, and laughed, his face round, red, and clean-shaven. Most of the hair from his forehead was long gone. His neck wasn't visible. He could have been forty. He wore a military uniform, khaki, with medals dangling from the chest. Johnson mentioned that he was a foot shorter than the real Winston Churchill. His attendant, Johny, called him Chota Churchill. Johny sat outside the door in a starched white shirt and pants, doused in strong cologne. Many in the asylum community would have recognized that Johny had overcompensated for the smell of alcohol. It was a problem all too common among the staff.

"I will have to take your leave now but before that, well, you asked for a reader, and here—"

"Him!" Churchill looked at Gaitonde.

"I promise he can read—"

"It's wartime, we must sacrifice I see."

"I am the world's first cow psychologist, Mr. Churchill," Gaitonde stammered.

"And you are here? Hasn't the world milked me enough?" Churchill laughed.

"Sir, they—"

"Either you are in the wrong hospital, or I am in the wrong animal."

"Sir—"

"Are you Hindou?"

"Yes."

"An idolatrous religion, isn't it? You worship cows and have become a detective to hide it."

"Psychologist."

"Does it matter? Here it's all the same. Can the cow speak English?"

"If you train—"

"You know that I hate brown bread, don't you?" He laughed heartily. Gaitonde had begun to sweat profusely.

"He rarely stops. But let that not be your problem. You will read the first two pages from the beginning to the end, then leave. If he is violent call the attendant. He will be outside," Clark Gable said, pointing to Johny.

"Newspaper?" Gaitonde asked.

"Ah, newspaper. Yes, here it is," Dr. Johnson said. "The *Bombay*

Chronicle. He thinks he runs the *Times of India.* Last month he forced the reader to call the editor. 'Hello, Churchill speaking.' The editor thought it was a call from Mr. Churchill himself. He made some changes. This calling business became routine until the newspaper found out that the calls were made from the Asylum, and it wasn't some wartime camouflage. The readers never found out though. Then there's the *Free Press Journal.* He doesn't like that one at all. Brown money he says."

"Of course," Gaitonde said.

"Watch." Dr. Johnson prodded Little Churchill, "Sir! Sir! You are no longer the PM. It is Attlee now."

"How dare you, you bastard. Don't you see? We have planned this to avert a Russian attack. I am here, Attlee, or whoever he is, is there. I am being protected. Can't you see the guards, you fool? Now call that naked fakir," Churchill responded.

"The Russians fought on your side, Mr. Churchill."

"A mouse will fight on the side with the cheese."

"Anyways Gaitonde, we keep him. It's a thankless job . . . and this shell shock business . . . at least we should entertain ourselves. Take care. Keep it light," Johnson waved and left. There was something breezy about him, but also fatalistic—like he was at a picnic, it had rained, and he was trying to make the most of it.

Gaitonde picked up the newspaper. When he turned, Little Churchill was standing right next to him with a cane in his hand.

"Yes boy, you think you can read."

Gaitonde tried to say something. He couldn't. His hands shook. He darted under the cot.

"Come out you swine," Churchill said. Gaitonde began to pull the bedsheet from the cot.

Johny rushed in.

"Room five," he called out.

Johnson returned. Churchill was on his chair, legs on the sill, looking out. Johny and Johnson grabbed the shivering Gaitonde from underneath the cot and put him in a wheelchair. Johnson wheeled him to the gate. Ghose was already waiting for him.

GAITONDE COULDN'T READ a line since he had arrived some forty minutes ago in Little Churchill's room.

". . . then Roosevelt said, 'a beautiful thing about America is that we have freedom of speech. Anybody can stand in front of the White House and say, 'Roosevelt is a piece of shit,' and nobody would pay any attention.' Then Stalin said, 'We too have freedom of speech in the Soviet Union. Anybody can stand in front of the Kremlin and say, 'Roosevelt is a piece of shit,' and no one would say anything.'" Churchill laughed until his cheeks turned red.

Gaitonde nodded.

"Stalin had a stock of jokes I tell you. He would go on and on, vodka, cigar, and jokes. I am sure that the KGB wrote them for him to make him popular. Whatever he is, the man knows how to fight. That's why I like him. He's not like Gandhi. Give me Bose over Gandhi any time, he's a worthy opponent. If I were an Indian, I would have shot the first Englishman in the face. If Britain had Gandhi, she would have been overrun by everyone, the French, the Germans, the Russians. Give me Dhingra. Now, that man is a true patriot. Assassinating the English in their own lair. Do you know what Dhingra said during the trial before he was dangling on the rope, 'If it is patriotic for an Englishman to fight the German, then it is patriotic for an Indian to fight the English.' Do you know what Gandhi said in response, 'The analogy is fallacious. If the Germans were to invade the Britishers, the British would only kill the invaders.' So Gandhi agrees that the English are not invaders, doesn't he? This is the kind of infantile man who negotiates for India. We bloody destroyed half the world in a war."

Little Churchill rose and banged his fists against the table. The pile of papers and files jumped and fell to the floor. Amid the scatter, a letter addressed from father to son took flight. Its weight delivered it under the cot where Gaitonde too had run for cover. The letter and Gaitonde met for a fleeting moment, exchanging glances, before Churchill grabbed the letter—

"You should be ashamed of your slovenly, happy-go-lucky, harum-scarum style of work. . . .

You are always behind. . . .

The teachers complain incessantly about you. . . .

You are a failure. . . .

You will degenerate into a shabby, unhappy, and futile existence."

DR. GHOSE diagnosed Gaitonde with cow mania. However, he did not settle on a treatment plan.

"TWO AND A HALF MILLION Indians served in the British Army. They fought the Azad Hind Sena. Eight million Indians took part in the war effort. Indians diverted all their cloth and shoe production to the war to support us. They listened to me, not to Gandhi. They love me more than they love Gandhi. Do you hear me! I taught the Indians to be brave. I created the Indian nation."

Johny and Dr. Johnson entered the room to find Churchill screaming at the top of his lungs.

"What did you do?" Johnson looked at Gaitonde, grabbing a shaking Churchill and laying him on the bed. Johny pinned Churchill's hands to the cot. Another attendant held his legs. Johnson returned with a syringe and pushed the needed through Churchill's arm, before turning to Gaitonde. "What are you standing here for? Leave."

Churchill sat up again and continued his drowsy barrage. "Do you know how many men we lost because of one Archduke, a million. . . . Do you know how many men we lost in the second world war to stop one German man, our own cousin? Half a million. We value death, valor, bravery, not a puny man in rags. Pacifism is for the weak. . . . We shall fight. We shall never surrender. We don't fight for what is right. That we fight, makes it right. We fight for us. That makes it right." He banged his fists on the table. "You put me on enemy grounds. I am not going to climb the steps. I am going to shoot them. That is the difference between me and Gandhi. You can't colonize a race led by me." Churchill slurred, fell sideways on the cot, then screamed.

Johnson pressed his own ears.

"Stuff his mouth," Gaitonde said.

"How dare you," Johnson responded, then sighed, "How can I? After all he is Churchill."

Churchill's eyes shut and he began to murmur.

"We need a new treatment," Johnson muttered on his way out.

THE NEW ELECTROTHERAPY apparatus was placed in a cold grey room in the basement below the toolshed where a damp smell of urine permeated. A few days of training and testing helped the staff develop a five-step guide.

1. Strap the patient to the bed.
2. Stuff a ball of cotton into the mouth to prevent the patient from biting his tongue off.
3. Plug the headphone to the temple.
4. Shock one. Shock two. Done.
5. Clean up.

GAITONDE KNOCKED. Little Churchill did not respond. Gaitonde pushed the door open. Churchill was lying on the cot face down, crying. Gaitonde sat on the chair. He coughed. Churchill turned.

"Did you take my watch?" Churchill asked.

"No." Gaitonde looked at him petrified.

"Do you know how much that watch matters to me? It has been with me since I was ten. Do you understand? It's my father's. It's gold."

"I have never seen it, sir."

"You have no idea how far I can go for it. I can give my life. . . . When I was at Sandhurst, it fell in a stream, six feet deep. I plunged in and searched for it for hours. I couldn't find it. I got the entire area dredged. I still couldn't find it. I got two dozen soldiers. Ordered them to dig a new course for the stream. I had them re-route the entire stream. Do you hear me? I still did not find it. I sent a policeman to the local fire station, ordered them to bring a large pump. A dozen firemen. They drained the entire pond. There it was. At the bottom. My gold watch. My father's gold watch. Now it is gone again. I will find it no matter what. I will blow this entire place with dynamite. Do you hear me?"

Gaitonde began to sweat. He couldn't get a word out of his mouth.

"Do you understand?"

"He has asked that question to everyone, don't worry," Johny called from outside the door. "The watch doesn't exist."

Gaitonde stepped out, ran to the toilet, vomited, washed his face, rubbed his palms together to gather warmth. He was still short of breath when he returned to the corridor.

Churchill stepped out of the room. He looked at Johny and Gaitonde with furious implicating eyes, then turned to the narrow path with a hedge on either side that led to the backyard and walked headlong into a brown cow with white spots. She was usually there in the morning hours demanding stale chapati and salt. Churchill

Kulkarni

stood angry and confounded. He plopped to the ground. Tears gushed down his face. The cow looked at him, came closer, and licked his face a few times. Churchill sat blubbering while the cow stood still. Suddenly he embraced her. She let him as if it was routine in her life to be hugged by teary old men.

Johny, too, had tears in his eyes.

MIDNIGHT. The moon is missing. Owls are hooting. Crickets are pursuing their communal rhythms. Gaitonde is sitting in his dream world. It is a memory from more than two decades ago.

Wooden floors, shelves of leather-bound books, the sun shining through the windows, chairs occupied, a murmuring public room at the Royal Asiatic Society Library, and Guy Cowley delivering a lecture from the podium.

"The Western infant tends towards castration anxiety, which is normal. He protects what he has. In the East, it is the cow that animalizes the man. Hence, the native occupies this intermediate space between man and beast, which we term 'savage.' The cow is on all fours. Milking must be done on all fours. Picking cow dung and playing with it is done on all fours. The West gave up all these tasks as uncivilized. The negative olfactory experience contributed to this speedy dissociation. The Eastern association with the cow led to the abnormal retention of lower-order sensory perceptions such as taste, smell, and touch and prevented the emergence of vision as the dominant sense. Verticality and vision are the origins of civilizational progress. Both are more delayed among the natives and the cow is indeed responsible. For this reason of perpetual horizontality, the Hindu cannot conquer. It is the cow that transforms the Hindu to docility in contrast to the ingrained spirit of domination, vision, and verticality that forms part of the Western psyche. It is for this reason that the West has never been a subject race."

Gaitonde woke with the words, "Verticality hypothesis! Verticality hypothesis! Verticality hypothesis!" receding to the background like it was a chant that filled the whole library, and he was walking away from it—not simply walking away, but being led away with thick iron chains on his feet and a black cloth tied over his face.

LITTLE CHURCHILL remained hidden in a cloud of melancholy for the entire week. He would stare absentmindedly toward the tree in the yard. Gaitonde would read his pages. At the end of his reading, he would clear his throat. Churchill would rise from his stupor and raise his hand. Gaitonde would leave with a nod.

A new day of a new month. Gaitonde sat in Churchill's room following his weekly ritual. He read the first page, stopped. Churchill looked at him. Gaitonde stuttered, "Have you considered a cow?"

"In my diet?" Churchill asked.

"No, to feel better."

Kulkarni

"I had a dog . . . he was my best friend," Churchill began to tear up again. He covered his face with his palms, sniffling persistently. A few minutes passed. Gaitonde stepped closer to Churchill, then some more, and finally, with some trepidation, he placed his palm on Churchill's back. Churchill put his arm around Gaitonde's waist and wept. Gaitonde saw Johny at the door, gave him a long look, and Johny took off. Five minutes later, he walked back with the spotted brown cow. Churchill sat on the chair scratching the cow's neck.

"All I wanted was love."

"What do you mean Mr. Churchill?"

They shifted to the stairs that led to the backyard. The cow sat next to Churchill.

"I spent my childhood in boarding schools. My parents didn't want me." His eyes glistened.

"Weren't you close to your father?"

"He wouldn't visit. Once I had pneumonia. I was as close to death as a dry leaf. He didn't come, not even then. He would bark at me all the time. He thought I was a fool. He didn't come to see me even when he was in the same city as I was, in Brighton."

"Your mother?"

THIS GATHERING—Little Churchill, the spotted brown cow, Gaitonde, and Johny—became a ritual, a place for revelation.

"I would marry her if I could."

"I was a machine for them, not even a cow, a machine."

"A cow doesn't belong in an asylum," an agitated Clark Gable said one morning. The four remained seated. Clark Gable came closer. The cow rose. He held her horn to push her away. She turned, lifted her hind leg, kicked him in the groin. He fell to the ground. She stood, simply stood, neither sat nor left, then turned her face to the wall. Moments later, Johny took her rope, led her to the gate, and dropped her outside.

The brown cow wasn't seen in the European section again. Little Churchill returned to his white tablets. The old temperament returned to Little Churchill. Shortly after the cow's departure, he had leaped on Gaitonde with a piece of beef Wellington on his fork. He ran after him all around the room, laughing.

"I saved the world. I stood against the fascists. I stood against the Communists. I brought civilization to the East. Do you understand?"

"I brought food to the colonies. Do you hear me? Tell that to Roosevelt. Who controls India? The landlords! The oppressive industrialists! Does Roosevelt know that Gandhi is their stooge . . . thoroughly evil, our main enemy? He's feeding millions of hungry mouths with a spindle wheel like some old Russian witch."

Churchill's voice boomed into the courtyard.

"Workers will be the victims of the capitalists. Farmers will be the victims of the money lenders. I say to Roosevelt, let America manage half of India, let me manage the other half, we see who wins. I bet my title. Tell that Roosevelt, I am ready to wager my life. I am standing here, go tell him."

GAITONDE'S COW PURSUITS traveled with laughter to the rest of the asylum. They reached Dr. Ghose's ears. Apathy receded; earnestness took over.

At 4 p.m., Gaitonde was strapped to the bed.

At 4:05 p.m., he closed his eyes to moments of excruciating pain. His body turned limp. His tongue hung loose. He looked around to see if the doctor was present. It was all blurry. He slurred, again tried to say something, drooled, and drifted to sleep.

TWO POEMS

Njoku Nonso

(winner of the 2022 Boston Review *Annual Poetry Contest)*

"My Mother Called Me a Bastard I Stood Laughing Because the First Rule of the Job is to Have Sex" is a poem of inquiry and vulnerabilty. In the shadows between declaration and interrogation thrums a longing to know and be known, to remember.

—Donika Kelly, 2022 Boston Review Annual Poetry Contest judge

MY MOTHER CALLED ME A BASTARD I STOOD LAUGHING
BECAUSE THE FIRST RULE OF THE JOB
IS TO HAVE SEX

The seventh-largest country in the world, Nigeria, has Africa's highest caseload of depression, and ranks 15th in the world in the frequency of suicide, according to the World Health Organization (WHO). There are less than 150 psychiatrists in this country of 200 million, and WHO estimates that fewer than 10 percent of mentally ill Nigerians have access to the care they need.

—Al Jazeera

Mental illnesses sometimes run in families, suggesting that people who have a family member with a mental illness may be somewhat more likely to develop one themselves.

—WebMD

The trick is to worship the shadow of the thing
& not the thing itself. That's winnowing the ruin:
to water one's garden in the avalanche of a storming war.
Replace *garden* with *family history*.
Replace *storming war* with *generational curse*.
& a recondite hush bassets like an iridescent mist
whistling in the company of trees. Shards of glass
in the throat of a baby hummer. What stories
do we tell only in the dark to safekeep our existence?
What stories do we put down into the red earth
like the appendix of a bad mistake? In mid-199*,
three sisters were found un-alive, hanging
from a tree in a forest near River John. I have seen it all:
each of their faces blotched with laughter
on a monochrome photograph anchored to the brick-
wall of my family history. The proof of an existential chaos.
I have heard stories of women who snatch foundlings
by their hair & fling them across the room
like a misguided applause. Women who are afraid to make love
to their husbands at night for what they could become
in their rusting. Women who have lived & re-lived
numberless nights the journey to the end of the world.

The meds are working more than your prayers,
my mother scribbled in one of her pink little journals.
I understand the joke. I count the bottle of pills
on the room divider, the crest of my tongue, hunger-green.

A CONFERENCE OF LAST CARDS

Bring me the city whether the city surrenders or not.
What bridges have in common is a monument of letters
written in past tense. Sieve through the ache and noise.
The stones are endlessly weeping in the dark. Or is it
the bird-chatter of rain. O darling, are you writing
another poem about trees? No, not trees but ghosts
that live on trees and their legend of never-let-gos.
The sight of your blood makes me fever-sick. Never
hide a butcher's knife inside your wrist. You know
if we fuck our bodies hard enough, we might still
make heaven; you know if you had followed the doctor's
prescription, I wouldn't need to plant marigolds at your
burial site. Come closer, darling, let's keep partying
in the same city where those doctors could not save your
diseased kidney. Sweat buds ripening. Urine-blue stains
all over the floor. The spit-wet bone of our hunger, genderless
and spectacular. Another final rough nightstand before you perish.

Nonso

twenty-nine, and continued to write for the remainder of her short life, producing thousands upon thousands of manuscript pages.

Fourteen books, and of the thirteen that are available—Butler refused to allow her novel *Survivor* to be republished in her lifetime, believing it to be an unfinished embarrassment—there is not a whiff among them. Nine, *Kindred* included, are masterpieces. Even her "lesser" efforts are wonders of craft and the imagination. Everything Butler wrote—story, novel, science fiction, fantasy—is marked by her interest in racial politics, in the history of the African diaspora, in the ability for an individual, usually a woman, to survive bondage. It all hums with an unbending will, muted ferocity, and clear-eyed pessimism that is as close as Butler came to autobiography. Hers is a prophetic literature that is equal parts revelation and terror—what Maxine Hong Kingston once called stories "to grow up on." Before Wakanda become part of the idiolect, Butler was writing Wakandas. Unlike so much of the larger culture in those days (Marvel included), Butler never had problems imagining Black people with Wakanda-like superpowers; she just couldn't imagine that Black people with Wakanda-like superpowers would ever be benevolent.

Butler won a MacArthur Fellowship and a number of Nebula and Hugo Awards, but she never received the success or financial stability she longed for. During her lifetime all her books went out of print at one time or another. I can remember as late as 2000, at a gathering of African diasporic faculty, being asked to recommend a Black writer, and when I named Butler, only two of the dozen professors had ever heard of her, and only one had read her books. At the end of her life, when her reputation had grown, Butler was still worried about her finances, convinced that she would need to write another two novels in order to retire. She died before she could write those novels or enjoy her retirement.

Fortunately for readers everywhere, Butler's reputation has only grown since her untimely passing. She has inspired essays, anthologies, dissertations, monographs, scholarships, prizes and, of course, legions of readers and artists. For many of us in the African diaspora, Butler is as much a founding mother—Butler wrote a lot about founding mothers—as she is an Eshu figure who *opened the way*. Many of the young writers of color kicking ass in speculative fiction today are Octavia's brood, whether they know it or not.

Kindred has benefited the most from the Butler boom. The book is one of Beacon Press's best sellers, and in 2017 a graphic novel adaptation rocketed to number one on the *New York Times* bestseller list. Now it has reached TV. For years Butler fans debated how her novels would play on the screen, how "the studios" would translate or dilute, realize or corrupt, Butler's uniquely unflinching (to put it mildly) worldview. Hulu has given us one answer, but hopefully there will be many more to come.

The novel has a simple, horrifying conceit. In mid-seventies Los Angeles, Dana, a struggling Black writer, finds herself being repeatedly hurled back in time—sometimes with her white husband, Kevin, sometimes alone (she drags along anything she's touching). Every single time she time-jumps, Dana ends up in the antebellum South: to the very plantation her ancestors were enslaved. In other words, Dana is hurled through time straight into the maw of American slavery, with nothing to protect her but her wits, her fierce will to live, and, occasionally, her husband's white skin (he has to pretend to be her master). Each trip to the past increases Dana's peril, until at last, before she can escape for good, her slave ancestors nearly kill her.

Kindred is thus simultaneously a time-travel story and a neo-slave narrative. Butler literalizes what's implicit in the genre—after all, isn't every neo-slave narrative a time-travel story? But don't let the temporal hijinks confuse you: this is no *Terminator* fantasy; even 1962's *La Jetée* seems downright cheery by comparison. Kindred, for my money, is second only to Morrison's *Beloved* (1987) in approximating the insane everyday nightmare that was American slavery. How it ate flesh, how it ate souls, how it ate presents, how it ate futures. In Butler's deft hands every moment that Dana spends in the past is torqued with dread, with the imminence of arbitrary annihilation. The real question is not whether the violation will come—it will—or if it will kill you (always a possibility), but whether it will shatter your humanity forever.

Kindred, you see, is also a horror novel. (Then again, what neo-slave narrative *isn't?*) But it is a horror novel of a very particular kind. What gets quickly revealed is that Dana is summoned to the past every time her white ancestor's life is in peril. At any of these crux moments Dana could choose to let the young slaver die, kill-whitey style, but then Dana's ancestor Hagar would not have been born, and neither would have Dana. In other words: a Black woman has to keep a white slaver alive long enough for him to rape her ancestor into existence. As Canavan aptly describes it, "Dana, is alive *after* slavery and *despite* slavery, but also *because* of slavery, a compromised and morally fraught position that forces her to make deeply unpleasant choices in the name of preserving the circumstances that led to her own birth."

It is this impossibly vile "compromise" that is *Kindred*'s true heart of darkness. It demonstrates why Butler has many imitators, but no equals. The novel takes aim at the consolatory reflex among many in the African diaspora who insist that white supremacy is Other, is *whitey* (and friends)—reminding us, emphatically, gruesomely, that white supremacy is *us too*.

AS A DEVOTEE of Butler, who longs for the whole world to read her, I was rooting for the TV adaptation of *Kindred*. I figured that the producers would have to tone down the more radical edges of Butler's novel—because, Hollywood—but with brilliant playwright Branden Jacobs-Jenkins heading the development, there was a real chance they could preserve the core of Butler's vision, do something nervy and off-kilter. What I didn't expect is that they would undo so much of what made the novel unique and powerful.

The most obvious and perhaps the most unavoidable change is that the show has been set in the Now. Gone are the novel's Bicentennial critiques, its depiction of the era's aggressive racism. (Butler's '70s would cause *That '70s Show* to implode on contact.) Gone, too, are Dana's working-class struggles. In the novel Dana works at a low-skill job agency and is so broke she cannot afford to eat; in the show Dana is flush. We find out in the first episode that she has sold the Manhattan brownstone she inherited from her grandmother for a tidy sum and bought herself a bungalow in Silver Lake.

Díaz

That is not to say the Dana of the show doesn't have her challenges (besides, you know, the time traveling). Her new house brings with it a pair of villainous white neighbors who are Super Karens. Then there's her aunt Sarah, who reacts to Dana's time travel tales by trying to have her thrown into a psych ward, perhaps in an effort to seize the brownstone inheritance she believes is rightfully hers. And we haven't even talked about the show's strangest twist: it turns out that Dana's long dead mother is alive; she just time-traveled back to the plantation and got stuck there.

If this all seems overstuffed, that's because it is. Overstuffed and distracting. But all the departures wouldn't be so bad, would even be tolerable, had the show landed the slavery half of the story. After all, *Kindred*, like Dana herself, lives or dies by what happens on the Weylin plantation. Unfortunately for the viewer and the series itself, TV *Kindred*'s take on slavery is so desultory and diffused that Dana's troubles as an LA homeowner often end up coming off as more perilous than the brutality of the peculiar institution.

In the novel, no sooner does Dana land in the South than she has to fight for her very life; no matter how she prepares, what she brings with her, or Kevin's best efforts, Dana is always one misstep from annihilation—or worse. The show, however, presents the Southern plantation as a more forgiving place; the show lets Dana, and later Kevin, get away with all types of slips and impertinences that would have gotten Novel Dana slain. There are a few notable stabs at historical verisimilitude—enslaved children scrambling on the floor for oranges, a white child threatening Dana with smug impunity—but these moments pass quickly or are resolved in Dana's favor. We don't get any real sense of the hell that was plantation life; we barely spend any time with the enslaved people Butler took such pains to humanize. The show seems more interested in Kevin's relationship with Rufus's father Tom than in any of the half-dozen enslaved people it introduces. In the novel, Tom is a brutal slaver, but the show transforms him into a foolish bad father who speaks in a pseudo-courtly register and seems unable to register Kevin or Dana's strangeness, a fact the series sometimes plays up for yuks. By the time Tom bares his fangs, we're at the end of the season and it's far too little, too late.

The show seems to misunderstand—or, worse, reject—Butler's implacable rendition of the plantation as site of soul-ravaging precarity. Nothing is more emblematic of this rejection than Dana's mother—a character, mind you, the scriptwriters invented whole cloth for the series. Dana's mother has been stuck on the plantation for years, and yet when Dana is at last reunited with her and offers her a shot at finally getting back to her real life, Mom doesn't seem all that pressed to leave. She has to be *convinced*—not to leave, but to *consider* leaving. Which is just nuts.

The show ultimately does not live up to the premise and challenge of the novel. All the stuff happening in the present, the inertness of the plantation scenes, the glib conflation of today's injustices with yesterday's harms, should have tipped me off that while Dana ostensibly travels back in time, the show in the end doesn't. Not fully.

The novel is prescient in this regard, too. Dana herself points out how difficult it would be for television to capture the hell she is experiencing: "most of the people around Rufus know more about real violence than the screenwriters of today will ever know." Butler was no doubt speaking

Díaz

why there are   empty villages
surrounded   by bloodish-red water.
     where the girls

are taken to   after abduction. do they
return whole   when they're released.
     how many

families i've lost   to the crisis. how deep
have the traumas   clawed into my body.
     does living

in this country   make me feel like
a child with   an open wound
     getting baptized

in a salt lake.   if i think the silicon plate
in his chest   can repel bullets
     in case

they start shooting.   if i would like to go
somewhere i can   sleep & not be woken
     by the sound

of rounds   rushing out of firearms.
in response, i ask   if he can just shut the fuck up.

EXODUS

Amanda Rizkalla
(fiction)

THE VIGIL was at seven.

Moonlight scattered around the crowd like snow. Maria and the fifteen other girls in her grade huddled around each other, some of them crying, sniffling, rubbing their noses red with wads of tissues. The mothers were whispering. The fathers looked on, silent.

Even in the dark, Maria could see posters of Nina's face flapping around the town like wild sails, stapled into wooden telephone poles, taped over storefronts with blue painter's tape. The posters were printed on high-gloss paper so reflective it was like looking at a mirror, and even at night people had to squint to walk past them.

"I can look for her, too, you know," Maria had said earlier, tugging on her mom's jacket at the community center. While Maria's mom handed plastic water bottles one by one to the search party, and while her older brother, Tomas, zipped up a bright yellow hazard vest over his chest to join them, Maria looked at the stack of posters in her hands, at Nina's light eyes, her hair pinned back by a gold and black barrette. Maria had given the barrette to Nina for her birthday. She had one to match. It was in her pocket.

"I can help," Maria said. "I'll be safe."

Maria's mom ignored her, rummaging in a bag for more water bottles.

Because the sun had already set, the search only lasted an hour. "No use in other people getting lost," the mayor said, switching off his walkie-talkie. Nina's mom corrected him: "Not lost. Missing. *Missing.*"

Now, at the vigil, the mayor cleared his throat before taking the microphone off the stand. The cord coiled like a thin, black snake around his shoes. He said that the search party, with their bloodhounds and megaphones and night-vision goggles, came up empty. "So why don't we have a moment of silence?"

After a minute, the mayor handed the microphone to Nina's mom.

She shook her head.

He insisted, nudging it toward her.

"Oh," she said, untangling her foot from the cord. "Thanks for coming." She rubbed her eyes with her sleeve. "Please, if you can—tomorrow. I'll be here tomorrow. We can start at five. I'll be here earlier than that, but we can start then. I don't know what else to say," she said, looking at the mayor, then back out at the crowd. "Her favorite color's purple. She loves to dance." She reached into her bag. "This is her," she said, unfolding a poster. "Thank you."

Maria wiped her nose. The tissue in her hand looked like a crumpled white carnation.

THAT NIGHT, walking up the squeaky, wood-splintered stairs to their apartment, Maria's mom said they would wake up at 4:30 tomorrow morning to make it to the community center by 5:00. She made Tomas and Maria sleep in her bedroom, stretching a heavy quilt over the three of them. "And no sleep-talking," she said, looking at Tomas.

Maria closed her eyes to make the room dark, the nightlight pulsing yellow beside her. There was the humming of the fence nearby, the drone of crickets' song, the whack of the tree branch against the storm gutters. She fluffed up her pillow. Tossed. Turned. She looked at the clock, then tried to make herself yawn.

"Mom, do you think Nina—" she started, trailing off. "Never mind."

Her mom rolled over to face her. "I think she'll be back before you know it."

"In time for my birthday?"

"In time for your birthday."

FOR A WEEK, people wore different shades of purple—lavender, violet, plum. The janitor painted the handle of his mop a deep fuchsia. Even the old librarian, who lost her twins in a house fire decades ago and refused to wear anything but black—who had replaced her furniture and curtains and plates with black couches and drapes and china—wrapped a pale purple scarf around her neck.

Rizkalla

Ms. Dane, Maria's fourth-grade teacher, said wearing Nina's favorite color might help her come home. Maria did not think that was true, but did it anyway, the same way she avoided cracks on the sidewalk for her mom's sake. Just in case.

By then, the local news channel had dedicated a nightly segment to Nina's disappearance, using full-screen terrain maps to show which areas had been searched that day, reporting on tips they had received through an anonymous tip line. Every night, before the weather forecast, a sad but serious news anchor would give an update, saying there was nothing substantial to report—but stay tuned for the weather. It was the town's first disappearance.

"Does anyone happen to know some of Nina's other favorite things? Favorite food, maybe?" Ms. Dane asked the class on the eighth day, tapping her chin with a pencil while she sat on top of her desk, ankles crossed.

Just in case, Maria thought. She raised her hand.

"Yes?"

"Persimmons," Maria said. "She brings one to lunch every day."

"Brought, you mean," one of the boys at the back of the classroom said, snickering. She turned to look at him. Nathan. To think Nina had a crush on him. Her eyes were too puffy to glare at him—the glare would be blurry, hazy—so she just looked at him until he looked away, uncomfortable.

"Cut it out, Nate," Ms. Dane said before looking back at Maria. "Persimmons? Alright."

The mayor arranged for it. Wicker baskets full of persimmons appeared around town: on the doorsteps of apartments, by the central water fountain, in the outstretched hands of the marble cherub statue by town hall. The persimmons were as shiny and round as ornaments, like someone had polished each one by hand. "For Nina only. Do not eat," read a note attached to each basket with a zip tie.

Maria hated seeing them. She hated how, by the eleventh day, all the persimmons rotted and the red-orange flesh stank up the streets—a sickly sweet, old towel smell. She hated how the white grubby worms inched their way through the fruit, carving finger-sized tunnels, gorging themselves so large they could no longer fit through the holes. She could hardly breathe without inhaling a few fruit flies.

"Alright, alright," said the mayor at the weekly town hall, after the townspeople presented him with a signed petition. "We'll remove them. I was just trying to help."

ON THE NINETEENTH DAY, it rained.

"Look," Tomas said, pointing out the window in the living room. Maria walked over from the kitchen, setting her glass on the dining table.

The posters.

They had fallen—soaked, sagging down from their staples, in wads on the street. Nina's face lay in wet clumps along the sidewalk. People stepped on the posters as they crossed the street, crosshatching black shoe prints over them, stamping them with mud. There were blue peels of tape. Some of the posters ripped, fragmenting her face. It was too much, seeing Nina's eye here, half of her smile there, in torn shreds.

Maria's mom shut the curtains. The living room lost its light.

"Don't worry," she said, pulling Maria close in the dark. "We'll put up more tomorrow."

MARIA DID NOT know Noreen.

All she knew was her picture, which was pinned over Nina's now, all over town. Laminated in case of rain. She had long brown hair. Blue eyes a few shades lighter than Nina's—clear like pool water. She looked serious in her picture, lawyer-like, her arms crossed over her chest. A hint of a smile, there, on her upper lip. A pink suggestion of one.

The town's theory was alphabetical.

"It's the letter 'N,'" Maria heard people say, approaching each other on the bus. She slung her backpack over her shoulder and looked out the window, at the A-frame houses that blurred as the bus drove past them, at the tulip-specked lawns, trying to contort her face to make it seem like she was not listening. "Both of their names start with the same letter," they said, clinging to the handrails as the bus jolted forward. "That has to be it."

At school, Ms. Dane assured the class that the theory was nonsense, although privately, she pulled aside three girls—Natalia, Natasha, and Nancy—and told them to take extra caution. After the recess bell rang, she handed each of them a small can of pepper spray and took them outside to show them how to use it.

"Aim, then spray. Okay girls?" she heard Ms. Dane say. "Aim for the eyes."

Maria heard the hiss of the spray can, saw white clouds burst from the pinhole-sized nozzles. Ms. Dane and the girls coughed and coughed. It sounded like they were gasping for breath, with their sharp, sudden, half-full intakes of air.

"Excellent," Ms. Dane said, hand over her mouth, wheezing.

THE TOWN wore blue. Noreen's favorite color.

Sea glass, midnight, navy, denim, indigo, cobalt.

Maria wore purple.

THE MORNING of her birthday, Maria sat across from a stack of blackberry-pecan pancakes, maple syrup dripping down the sides in amber globs, pooling on the plate. She watched as her mom stuck a waxy candle in the center of the stack. The lighter clicked. The wick turned black. A crumb of light. It reminded her of the vigil—the way the candle flames licked the air like small, orange tongues.

"Maria?" her mom said. "Earth to Maria."

"Sorry."

"I was asking if you had a birthday wish."

Maria nodded. She blew out the candle.

"So, listen, I know this isn't the birthday we had in mind, but we'll make it work," her mom said, pouring a glass of milk for her brother. "Want to open your present now or later?" She set the glass on the table, then reached underneath to pull out a striped silver gift bag with an eruption of red tissue paper on top.

"Later," Maria said, poking at her pancakes with a fork. She was not hungry. Most of her classmates' parents had called earlier that morning, saying they did not think it was safe for their kids to go to her birthday party, with Nina and Noreen and all. They said they would send birthday presents with their kids on Monday. "Tell her happy birthday for us," they said before hanging up. Above her, balloons clustered on the ceiling, their black ribbon tails dangling. There were two dozen cupcakes frosted, sprinkled, on the kitchen counter, which Tomas and her mom had spent all night making. She remembered how the two of them looked before bed last night—their pants dusted with icing sugar, sprinkles caught in their eyelashes.

"More for us," her mom had said after the first few calls, licking the frosting off a cupcake. It looked like a lump of white putty on her tongue.

Maria pushed her plate in front of her, then put her head down on the wooden table. Nathan's birthday party had been the previous weekend and all the boys, including Tomas, were allowed to go. They played capture the flag in the mud all afternoon, their cheeks seared red in the hot orange sunlight, then ran to the lake to wash off, looking for frogs, picking them up by their slimy green legs and dangling them over the rippling water. Tomas said his frog caught a fly while it was upside down, a fast pink tongue darting out mid-croak. He said he heard the crunch of the fly's wings. A faint buzzing from the frog's belly. Then they had cake. Red velvet. They sang Happy Birthday twice, an encore. Meanwhile, Maria and the rest of the girls remained at home.

"What about the boys? Are they coming?" she asked.

Her mom looked down, then shook her head. "I don't think so."

"But that's not fair." Maria stood up.

"I know it's not, mija, but—hey, hey, stop, where are you going?"

Maria ran to her room then slammed the door behind her. It rattled in the doorframe.

She threw herself onto her bed, then curled up on her side, her right ear pressed to her pillow. She reached down and pulled the low drawer of her bedside table open. Inside was her journal, her barrette, and a ticket stub from the zoo. She took the ticket stub in her hands, folding and unfolding it. Everyone in their grade had gone to Nina's birthday party a few months ago. Her parents had reserved a booth at the zoo, by the hippopotamus exhibit. A baby hippopotamus had recently been born—slippery and small among the herd of solid-looking adults—and it was its first day on display. Maria, Tomas, and their mom helped Nina's parents pitch a large white tent over the booth. They spread plastic tablecloths over wooden folding tables, braided purple streamers overhead. There were boxes of pizza, aluminum trays of garlic bread, bowls full of salad. Maria placed a party hat on the seat of each chair.

She remembered how, after her classmates had arrived, a zookeeper rolled out a wooden crate full of watermelons on a dolly and told them to get in line, single file. He took a watermelon from the crate and tossed it into the pen with two hands. It split when it landed—pink flesh and black seeds in a slushy pile. Maria watched as a hippopotamus took both halves into its mouth and jutted its stubby teeth through the rind. "Who wants to try?" the zookeeper said, reaching into the crate for another watermelon.

"Me, me!" Nina had said.

"Alright, birthday girl goes first," he said, stooping down to her.

When everyone left, Nina's parents drove Maria to their house for a sleepover—just her and Nina. The girls changed into matching purple pajama dresses and watched a movie in the living room. Nina's parents brought snacks out on a tray and set it on the coffee table in front of them. Grapes, popcorn, and juice pouches. After the movie ended, they threw grapes into each other's mouths, pretending one was the zookeeper, and the other, the hippo, cheering each time they made it.

Maria looked at the ticket stub again. She placed it under her pillow.

ANNIE. Fifth grade. Freckles.

In the picture, her hair was braided into a fishtail, ending in a puffy, yellow, popcorn-like scrunchy.

CASSANDRA. Played the violin. Allergic to honeybees.

THREE OF THE FOUR missing girls had blue eyes.

"That's why we're doing this," the mayor said, handing each girl a cellophane-wrapped bag at the community center. Maria loosened the silky ribbon until it fell to the floor. Inside: a bottle of contact solution and a box of lenses. Maria turned over the box in her hands. She found a label on the side. The contacts were grey.

"But what if my daughter doesn't have blue eyes?" a mother in the crowd asked, standing up. Other mothers nodded in agreement, a sea of them, nodding.

"Doesn't matter," the mayor said, putting his hands in his pockets. "Cassandra had brown eyes and she's still missing. We're doing this to eliminate possibilities. In case the kidnapper has a pattern."

"But—" the mother said.

"I'll take questions after," he said, putting his hand up. She sat down, exchanging frantic looks with the other mothers around her. "Alright, so, the optometrists have volunteered to help. Raise your hands, optometrists." They did. "Great. They'll show you how to put them in. If you'll just come over here, girls," he said, pointing to a long row of plastic tables, folding chairs scooted in.

It took Maria three tries to get her contacts in. She blinked to help them settle, aware of them every time her gaze shifted. The optometrist wore a white coat over dark pants and a plaid button-down shirt, with powdery blue gloves stretched over his hands. He handed her a small oval mirror. His eyes were green.

"What do you think?"

Maria shrugged, swallowing down a shriek. It was like looking at a stranger. Reflected back at her, she saw a girl with long, brown hair wearing a long-sleeved purple sweater. But the eyes. Pearls of fog, two of them, looking out at her. She put the mirror face down on the plastic table.

"It's not that bad," her mom said, bending down to her. "And anyway, it's just temporary."

DIANA.

LANEY.

MABLE.

STANDING IN FRONT of a telephone pole by the grocery store, Maria had to flip through a stack of stapled posters to find Nina's. When she found it, she noticed how much the poster had yellowed. Nina's teeth, which were white in real life, looked like kernels of corn, and her eyes were no longer blue, but a faded, sun-bleached green.

"I don't get it," Maria said, turning to her mom. "If we don't know what they look like, how will people be able to look for them?"

The day prior, the mayor announced that the city council would no longer be printing missing posters. "Until further notice, we'll be suspending that aspect of the search and rescue process," he said, adjusting his tie in a public broadcast, blinking from the white flashes of press cameras. The printers—all of them—ran out of ink. It would be weeks until the next shipment. For now, the mayor said they would be using news broadcasts and word-of-mouth descriptions if any more girls went missing.

"They'll get more ink soon," her mom said, straightening out a bent corner of Nina's poster. She took Maria's hand in hers, then swung it forward, toward the auditorium.

"Do I have to go?" Maria said a few minutes later, standing in front of the entrance.

Her mom kissed her forehead. "I'll be back at five to come get you."

The self-defense classes were compulsory. The mayor kept attendance himself, making sharp, red checkmarks on a notepad attached to a clipboard. Maria and the rest of the girls, the youngest of them five years old, sat in the auditorium while the slideshow flashed before them. She took notes, writing down the seven types of basic kicks—axe, back, crescent, front, push, roundhouse, and side—and sketched a stick-figure drawing to the left of each one. She wrote down how to shove using your body weight, how to punch, where to punch, "speed vs. accuracy," how to squirm out of a grasp, how to call for help, how to yell for it—it had to be a yell.

They set out a blue tarp in the parking lot and provided each girl with a Styrofoam dummy to practice. "Let's call him Bob," the presenter, a woman in her twenties wearing loose gym clothes, said. "Now let's say Bob comes up to you. What do you do?"

Maria kicked into it, punched it, shoved it, dug her fingers into its eyes, while the girls around her did the same. They yelled for help. Front-kicked and back-kicked. The woman called time. Styrofoam beads flurried around them, crumbled corners of Bob landed by their feet, here, there, everywhere. Maria had punched his nose out. It sat, nostrils up, on the tarp, while she caught her breath.

TIFFANY. Lena.

MEREDITH. Noor. Crystal.

SARAH. Hazel. Erin. Kayley. Mia. Peyton. Lily. Melinda.

THE TRIMMINGS BEGAN the following week, gleams of shiny black hair, brown ringlet curls, blonde waves all swept into a pile on the floor. Strands floated in the wind like dandelion wisps. Almost all the missing girls had medium or long hair. If they all had short hair, it might make them less of a target.

Maria looked at the shears—at the hairdresser's fingers bent inside the metal loops—then closed her eyes. She heard the crisp sound of the first snip. Her whole life, she had worn her hair long. Her mom only let her cut it a handful of times, and even then, it was the smallest of trimmings, for split ends only. Maria's abuela had long hair that shined its way down to her calves and Maria was determined to grow her own longer. After a few minutes, the hairdresser unclipped the black cape she had draped over Maria's chest, and sent her on her way.

"No mirror?" she asked.

"No time," the hairdresser said, shaking her head. "Who's next?"

Maria lifted herself off the chair. The hair pile was a large, shampoo-scented tumbleweed. The janitor swept her hair into a neat pile, then scooted it outside, toward the tumbleweed. Birds fluttered down, circling it. Some disappeared into its center, their twiglike feet poking out. She walked toward it. A yellow bird, a canary, picked at it with its small beige beak. It nibbled on a lock of her hair, then grabbed it, trotting away.

Maria followed it.

Past the bushes, through the gate. To her right, boys played in the baseball field, with their wind tousled, any-length hair, their any-colored eyes. The canary fluffed up its chest then flew away. She ran behind it. Fifty feet ahead, it swooped up to a nest. She could see three or four small pink heads bolting up above the nest, which was woven into a corner where a tree branch met another. The canary stuffed the hair lock around the chicks, then sat on top of them. The chirping stifled. Maybe she could climb the tree.

Then she felt someone grab her wrist.

Maria kicked herself free—a stiff crescent kick—and landed on the floor, by the base of the tree. She looked up to see a security guard keeled over himself. A walkie-talkie blipped. He asked her, groaning, what on earth she thought she was doing, wandering around on her own. "Don't you know any better? With all that's going on, you would think—"

She ran back to the salon, where her mom was waiting for her.

PAIGE. Luna. Charlotte. Stephanie. Olivia. Rena. Michelle. Teagan. Annamarie. Ynes. Emelia. Angelina. Ella. Alessandra. Stephanie. Irina. Jasmine. Robin. Aubrey. Lisa. Sienna. Blair. Maya. Victoria. Nova. Clara. Lumi. Regina. Tanya. Riley. Lili. Leilani. Alana. Grace. Jimena. Zoey. Hazel. Andrea. Kathleen. Shannon. Jaqueline. Lexi. Terry. Annalise. Suzie. Vera. Caterina. Josefina. Gina. Alyssa. Jacinta. Camryn. Madison. Donna. Julie. Alison. Amy. Ashlee. Chloe. Sarah Eliana. Kimberley. Lucy Rose. Miriam. Dina. Allie. Reina. Wendy. Joy. Leah. Arya. Yolanda. Sophie. Evelynn. Paula. Celeste. Sophia. Sarah Helen. Amber. Alexa. M. Melissa. Brandi. Charlotte. Amy. Alexis. Erin. Chloe. Tori. Lucy Shelly. Emma. Margaret. Jessica. Mariana. Kelly. Cate. Ella. Rosalie. Olivia. Ashley. Amelia. Krista. Brenda. Jody. Emilia. Elsie. Lauren. Carolyn. Elena. Eleanor. Zuri. Ellie. Linda. Arianna. Candace. Marta. Angelica. Michelle. Selena. Lydia. Sabrina. Rachel. Brianna. Kiara. Tina. Leia. Annie. Lana. Kimmy. Anne. Holly. Elizabeth. Mary. Sandy. Patricia. Victoria.

Molly. Willow. Nicole. Morgan. Teresa. Ruth. Beatrice. Christina. Rebecca. Celine. Adelina. Leslie. Mina. Jennifer. Stella. Caitlin. Heather. Joanna. Erica. Beverly. Grace. Kendall. Cheryl. Karen. Aly. Bailey. Dawn. Isobel. Brooke. Nicole. Priscila. Anamaria. Lilianna. Paola. Fiona. Taylor. Jill. Laurie. Nadia. Hayley. Faith. Sarah.

THE MAYOR DISLIKED the nickname the town had come up with. "They're not like bird cages at all. They're much, much bigger," he said, slamming his hand on his desk.

His assistant cleared her throat.

"What?" the mayor said.

"Nothing, I—" She looked down at her clipboard. "It's just they're a little like bird cages, sir," the assistant, a woman in her thirties, said. "I mean, they're domed. Metal bars."

The mayor groaned. He reached for the blue binder on the desk in front of him, white post-it notes sticking out like little flags. He flipped it open. "I don't know what else to do," he said. "We've tried everything in the handbook. Every. Last. Thing."

The mayor was not stupid. He knew what people were saying about him. When he first heard the rumors, whispers that people suspected him, of all people, as the kidnapper, he promptly offered public tours of the mayoral estate. He ordered the staff to open every door, every cupboard, to show the town that the girls were not there. The only girl at his estate was his granddaughter, Millie, who had been living with him for the year while her parents were on sabbatical in Europe. After touring the estate, lifting loose floorboards and double-checking cabinets, the townspeople seemed content enough, though that did not stop the whispers.

"Sir?" the assistant said, tapping his shoulder. "It's 6:45. We should probably head over."

He looked at the clock, rose up out of his chair, then straightened his suit.

"I'll meet you there. I'm going to say goodbye to Millie," he said, tucking his binder under his arm. He walked up the stairs to the guest room, where his granddaughter was staying. The room was beach-themed, with painted clams and dried starfish in a decorative bowl by the window, next to soy candles carved in the arched shape of dolphins. Outside, by the balcony, a wind chime made of sand dollars swayed, a tweed fishnet draped over the corner of the window. After it became unsafe for the girls to go outside, he commissioned an interior designer to decorate the room this way, paying extra for authentic conch shells. Millie loved the ocean. He had been there the first time she had seen it, years ago, when she was a baby. He remembered how her little fingers picked up a fistful of sand then let it blow away in the wind.

"I'm heading out, sweetheart," the mayor said, poking his head through the doorway. "I'll see you after the town hall, alright?"

Millie was sitting on the floor, propped up on her elbows and leaning over a puzzle in the safety enclosure when he walked in. The way she perked up each time he came to visit—it made him sick. He would do better, he decided. He would see her more often.

"You'll help me with the puzzle when you come back?" she asked, smiling.

He kissed her cheek through the metal bars. They were cold against his face. "Of course."

THAT EVENING, Maria laid down on the floor of her bedroom, looking out of the domed bars. The lukewarm sunlight flushed the room a soft pink, casting vertical shadows across her face. Her room was empty except for the enclosure—no rugs or furniture or books. She had not been outside in weeks.

Maria knew it was summer now because the sun took its time to set, crawling its way down the ladder of the horizon rung by rung. And she knew it was Thursday because she could hear footsteps outside, the click of heeled boots, the thwack of sandals. For weeks now, she watched as the fathers, mothers, and sons flocked to the community center for the weekly town hall, Thursday after Thursday. Each time they left, she could hear the girl in the apartment above her rattle her safety enclosure, shaking it and shaking it until the other girls in the complex did the same, metal scraping against wood, metal rattling metal. They rattled so much and for so long, Maria wondered if the building itself shook, too. She hugged her knees to her chest.

The townspeople, who could hear the rattling all the way from the community center, found it disturbing. And so last week, it was decided that the girls would be allowed to request one personal item

Your death certificate says
"nervous type" and "tuberculosis."
Life Magazine says the asylum was "Bedlam"—
says you were most likely restrained
for days in leather cuffs,
or put in the "dungeon"
or, the historians say, worse because you were Black, and

my grandmother tells me she loved you fiercely
in the way she reaches for me when your name
is spoken.

A martyr, the first miracle—
Aunt Lillie, my hand in yours,
writing this.

The second—you alive, white
collared and dressed in black.

THE NEW MORAL MATHEMATICS
Kieran Setiya

"SPACE IS BIG," wrote Douglas Adams in *The Hitchhiker's Guide to the Galaxy* (1979). "You just won't believe how vastly, hugely, mind-bogglingly big it is. I mean, you may think it's a long way down the road to the chemist's, but that's just peanuts to space."

Time is big, too—even if we just think on the timescale of a species. We've been around for approximately 300,000 years. There are now about 8 billion of us, roughly 15 percent of all humans who have ever lived. You may think that's a lot, but it's just peanuts to the future. If we survive for another million years—the longevity of a typical mammalian species—at even a tenth of our current population, there will be 8 trillion more of us. We'll be outnumbered by future people on the scale of a thousand to one.

What we do now affects those future people in dramatic ways: whether they will exist at all and in what numbers; what values they embrace; what sort of planet they inherit; what sorts of lives they lead. It's as if we're trapped on a tiny island while our actions determine the habitability of a vast continent and the life prospects of the many who may, or may not, inhabit it. What an awful responsibility.

This is the perspective of the "longtermist," for whom the history of human life so far stands to the future of humanity as a trip to the chemist's stands to a mission to Mars.

Oxford philosophers William MacAskill and Toby Ord, both affiliated with the university's Future of Humanity Institute, coined the word "longtermism" five years ago. Their outlook draws on utilitarian thinking about morality. According to utilitarianism—a moral theory developed by Jeremy Bentham and John Stuart Mill in the nineteenth century—we are morally required to maximize expected aggregate well-being, adding points for every moment of happiness, subtracting points for suffering, and discounting for probability. When you do this, you find that tiny chances of extinction swamp the moral mathematics. If you could save a million lives today or shave 0.0001 percent off the probability of premature human extinction—a one in a million chance of saving at least 8 trillion lives—you should do the latter, allowing a million people to die.

Now, as many have noted since its origin, utilitarianism is a radically counterintuitive moral view. It tells us that we cannot give more weight to our own interests or the interests of those we love than the interests of perfect strangers. We must sacrifice everything for the greater good. Worse, it tells us that we should do so by any effective means: if we can shave 0.0001 percent off the probability of human extinction by *killing* a million people, we should—so long as there are no other adverse effects.

But even if you think we are allowed to prioritize ourselves and those we love, and not allowed to violate the rights of some in order to help others, shouldn't you still care about the fate of strangers, even those who do not yet exist? The moral mathematics of aggregate well-being may not be the whole of ethics, but isn't it a vital part? It belongs to the domain of morality we call "altruism" or "charity." When we ask what we should do to benefit others, we can't ignore the disquieting fact that the others who occupy the future may vastly outnumber those who occupy the present, and that their very existence depends on us.

From this point of view, it's an urgent question how what we do today will affect the further future—urgent especially when it comes to what Nick Bostrom, the philosopher who directs the Future of Humanity Institute, calls the "existential risk" of human extinction. This is the question MacAskill takes up in his new book, *What We Owe the Future*, a densely researched but surprisingly light read that ranges from omnicidal pandemics to our new AI overlords without ever becoming bleak.

Like Bostrom, MacAskill has a big audience—unusually big for an academic philosopher. Bill Gates has called him "a data nerd after my own heart." In 2009 he and Ord helped found Giving What We Can, an organization that encourages people to pledge at least 10 percent of their income to charitable causes. With our tithe, MacAskill holds, we should be utilitarian, aggregating benefits, subtracting harms, and weighing odds: our 10 percent should be directed to the most effective charities, gauged by ruthless empirical measures. Thus the movement known as Effective Altruism (EA), in which MacAskill is a leading figure. (Peter Singer is another.) By one estimate, about $46 billion is now committed to EA. The movement counts among its acolytes such prominent billionaires as Peter Thiel, who gave a keynote address at the 2013 EA Summit, and now disgraced cryptocurrency exchange pioneer Sam Bankman-Fried, who became a convert as an undergraduate at MIT.

Effective Altruists need not be utilitarians about morality (though some are). Theirs is a bounded altruism, one that respects the rights of others. But they are inveterate quantifiers, and when they do the altruistic math, they are led to longtermism and to the quietly radical arguments of MacAskill's book. "Future people count," MacAskill writes:

> There could be a lot of them. We can make their lives go better. This is the case for longtermism in a nutshell. The premises are simple, and I don't think they're particularly controversial. Yet taking them seriously amounts to a moral revolution.

The premises are indeed simple. Most people concerned with the effects of climate change would accept them. Yet MacAskill pursues these premises to unexpected ends. If the premises are true, he argues, we should do what we can to ensure that "future civilization will be *big*."

MacAskill spends a lot of time and effort asking *how* to benefit future people. What I'll come back to is the moral question *whether* they matter in the way he thinks they do, and *why*. As it turns out, MacAskill's moral revolution rests on contentious, counterintuitive claims in "population ethics."

WHEN IT COMES to the *how*, MacAskill is fascinating—if, at times, alarming. Since having a positive influence on the long-term future is "a key moral priority of our time," he writes, we need to estimate what influence our actions will have. It is difficult to predict what will happen over many thousands of years, of course, and MacAskill doesn't approach the task alone: his book, he tells us, relies on a decade of research, including two years of fact-checking, in consultation with numerous "domain experts."

The long-term value of working for a given outcome is a function of that outcome's significance (what MacAskill calls its "average value added"), its persistence or longevity, and its contingency—the extent to which it depends on us and wouldn't happen anyway.

Among the most significant and persistent determinants of life for future generations, MacAskill argues, are the values we pass on to them. And values are often contingent. MacAskill takes as a case study the abolition of slavery in the nineteenth century. Was it, he asks, "more like the use of electricity—a more or less inevitable development once the idea was there?" or "like the wearing of neckties: a cultural contingency that became nearly universal globally but which could quite easily have been different?" Slavery had been abolished in Europe once before, in the late middle ages, only to return with a vengeance. Was it destined to decline again? MacAskill cites historian Christopher Leslie Brown, writing in *Moral Capital* (2006): "In key respects the British antislavery movement was a historical accident, a contingent event that just as easily might never have occurred." Values matter to the long-term future, and they are subject to intentional change.

From here we lurch to the alarming: MacAskill is worried about the development of artificial general intelligence (AGI), capable of performing as wide a range of tasks as we do, at least as well or better. He rates the chances of AGI arriving in the next fifty years no lower than one in ten. The risk is that, if AGI takes over the world, its creators' vision may be locked in for a very long time. "If we don't design our institutions to govern this transition well—preserving a plurality of values and the possibility of desirable moral progress," MacAskill writes, "then a single set of values could emerge dominant." The results might be dystopian: What if the AGI that rules the world belongs to a fascist government or a rapacious trillionaire?

MacAskill calls for better regulation of AI research to preserve space for reflection, open-mindedness, and political experimentation. Most of us would not object. But, as is often the case in discussions of AI—and despite the salience of contingency—MacAskill tends to treat the progress of technology as a given. We can hope to govern the transition to AGI well, but the transition is certainly coming. What we do "could affect what values are predominant when AGI is first built," MacAskill notes—but not whether it is built at all. Like the philosopher Annette Zimmermann, I hope that isn't true.

MacAskill may be reconciled to AGI, himself, by the hope that it will address another long-term problem: the threat of economic and technological stagnation. Again, his argument is both fascinating and alarming. "For the first 290,000 years of humanity's existence," MacAskill writes, "global growth was close to 0 percent per year; in the agricultural era that increased to around 0.1 percent, and it accelerated from there after the Industrial Revolution. It's only in the last hundred years that the world economy has grown at a rate above 2 percent per year." But it can't go on forever: "if current growth rates continued for just ten millennia more, there would have to be ten million trillion times as much output as our current world produces for *every atom* that we could, in principle, access"—that is, for every atom within ten thousand light years of Earth. "Though of course we can't be certain," MacAskill drily concludes, "this just doesn't seem possible."

There is evidence that technological process has already slowed down outside the areas of computation and AI. The rate of growth in "total factor productivity"—our ability to get more economic output from the same input—is declining, and according to a recent study by economists at Stanford and the London School of Economics, new ideas are increasingly scarce. MacAskill illustrates this neatly, imagining how your life would change in fifty years. When you go from 1870 to 1920, you get running water, electricity, a telephone, and perhaps a car. When you go 1970 to 2020, you get a microwave oven and a bigger TV. The only dramatic shifts are in computing and communications. Without the magic bullet of AGI, through which we might build unlimited AI workers in R&D, MacAskill fears that we are doomed to stagnation, perhaps for hundreds or thousands of years. But from his perspective, if it's not permanent, and people don't wish they'd never been born, it's not so bad. The worst things about stagnation, for MacAskill, are the dangers of misguided value lock-in and of extinction or permanent collapse.

Here we come, at last, to existential risks: asteroid collisions, which we might not detect; lethal pandemics, which might be bio-engineered; World War III, which might turn nuclear; and climate change, which might accelerate through feedback in the climate system. MacAskill applauds NASA's Spaceguard program, calls for better pandemic preparedness and biotech safety (experts, he notes, "put the probability of an extinction-level engineered pandemic this century at around 1 percent"), and supports a rapid shift to green energy.

But what is most alarming in his approach is how little he is alarmed. As of 2022, the *Bulletin of Atomic Scientists* set the Doomsday Clock, which measures our proximity to doom, at 100 seconds to midnight, the closest it's ever been. According to a study commissioned by MacAskill, however, even in the worst-case scenario—a nuclear war that kills 99 percent of us—society would likely survive. The future trillions would be safe. The same goes for climate change. MacAskill is upbeat about our chances of surviving seven degrees of warming or worse: "even with fifteen degrees of warming," he contends, "the heat would not pass lethal limits for crops in most regions."

This is shocking in two ways. First, because it conflicts with credible claims one reads elsewhere. The last time the temperature was six degree higher than preindustrial levels was 251 million years ago, in the Permian-Triassic Extinction, the most devastating of the five great extinctions. Deserts reached almost to the Arctic and more than 90 percent of species were wiped out. According to environmental journalist Mark Lynas, who synthesized current research in *Our Final Warning: Six Degrees of Climate Emergency* (2020), at six degrees of warming the oceans will become anoxic, killing most marine life, and they'll begin to release methane hydrate, which is flammable at concentrations of five percent, creating a risk of roving firestorms. It's not clear how we could survive this hell, let alone fifteen degrees.

The second shock is how much more MacAskill values survival in the long term over a decrease of suffering and death in the near future. This is the sharp end of longtermism. Most of us agree that (1) *world peace* is better than (2) *the death of 99 percent of the world's population*, which is better in turn than (3) *human extinction*. But how much better? Where many would see a greater gap between (1) and (2) than between (2) and (3), the longtermist disagrees. The gap between (1) and (2) is a temporary loss of population from which we will (or at least may) bounce back; the gap between (2) and (3) is "trillions upon trillions of people who would otherwise have been born." This is the "insight" MacAskill credits to the iconic moral philosopher Derek Parfit. It's the ethical crux of the most alarming claims in MacAskill's book. And there is no way to evaluate it without dipping our toes into the deep, dark waters of population ethics.

POPULATION ETHICISTS ask how good the world would be with a given population distribution, specified by the number of people existing at various levels of lifetime well-being throughout space and time. Should we measure by total aggregate well-being? By average? Should we care about distribution, rating inequitable outcomes worse? As MacAskill writes, population ethics is "one of the most complex areas of moral philosophy . . . normally studied only at the graduate level. To my knowledge, these ideas haven't been presented to a general audience before." But he gives it his best, and with trepidation, I'll follow suit.

Setiya

At the heart of the debate is what MacAskill calls "the intuition of neutrality," elegantly expressed by moral philosopher Jan Narveson in a much-cited slogan: "We are in favour of making people happy, but neutral about making happy people." The appeal of the slogan is apparent at scales both large and small. Suppose you are told that humanity will go extinct in a thousand years but also that everyone who lives will have a good enough life. Should you care if the average population each year is closer to 1 billion or 2? Neutrality says no. What matters is quality, not quantity.

Now suppose you are deciding whether to have a child, and you expect that your child would have a good enough life. Must you conclude that it would be better to have a child than not, unless you can point to some countervailing reason? Again, neutrality says no. In itself, adding an extra life to the world is no better (or worse) than not doing so. It's entirely up to you. It doesn't follow that you shouldn't care about the well-being of your potential child. Instead, there's an asymmetry: although it is not better to have a happy child than no child at all, it is worse to have a child whose life is not worth living.

Longtermists deny neutrality: they argue that it's always better, other things equal, if another person exists, provided their life is good enough. That's why human extinction looms so large. A world in which we have trillions of descendants living good enough lives is better than a world in which humanity goes extinct in a thousand years—better by a vast, huge, mind-boggling margin. A chance to reduce the risk of human extinction by 0.01 percent, say, is a chance to make the world an inconceivably better place. It's a greater contribution to the good, by several orders of magnitude, than saving a million lives today.

But if neutrality is right, the longtermist's mathematics rest on a mistake: the extra lives don't make the world a better place, all by themselves. Our ethical equations are not swamped by small risks of extinction. And while we may be doing much less than we should to address the risk of a lethal pandemic, value lock-in, or nuclear war, the truth is much closer to common sense than MacAskill would have us believe. We should care about making the lives of those who will exist better, or about the fate of those who will be worse off, not about the number of good lives there will be. According to MacAskill, the "practical upshot" of longtermism "is a moral case for space settlement," by which we could increase the future population by trillions. If we accept neutrality, by contrast, we will be happy if we can make things work on Earth.

An awful lot turns on the intuition of neutrality, then. MacAskill gives several arguments against it. One is about the ethics of procreation. If you are thinking of having a child, but you have a vitamin deficiency that means any child you conceive now will have a health condition—say, recurrent migraines—you should take vitamins to resolve the deficiency before you try to get pregnant. But then, MacAskill argues, "having a child cannot be a neutral matter." The steps of his argument, a *reductio ad absurdum*, bear spelling out. Compare having no child with having a child who has migraines, but whose life is still worth living. "According to the intuition of neutrality," MacAskill writes, "the world is equally good either way." The same is true if we compare having no child with waiting to get pregnant in order to have a child who is migraine-free. From this it follows, MacAskill claims, that having a child with recurrent migraines is as good an outcome as having a child without. That's absurd. In order to avoid this consequence, MacAskill concludes, we must reject neutrality.

But the argument is flawed. Neutrality says that having a child with a good enough life is on a par with staying childless, not that the outcome in which you have a child is equally good regardless of their well-being. Consider a frivolous analogy: being a philosopher is on a par with being a poet—neither is strictly better or worse—but it doesn't follow that being a philosopher is equally good, regardless of the pay.

A striking fact about cases like the one MacAskill cites is that they are subject to a retrospective shift. If you are planning to have a child, you should wait until your vitamin deficiency is resolved. But if you don't wait and you give birth to a child, migraines and all, you should love them and affirm their existence—not wish you had waited, so that they'd never been born. This shift explains what's wrong with a second argument MacAskill makes against neutrality. Thinking of his nephew and two nieces, MacAskill is inclined to say that the world is "at least a little better" for their existence. "If so," he argues, "the intuition of neutrality is wrong." But again, the argument is flawed. Once someone is born, you should welcome their existence as a good thing. It doesn't follow that you should have seen their coming to exist as an improvement in the world before they came into existence. Neutrality survives intact.

In rejecting neutrality, MacAskill leans toward the "total view" on which one population distribution is better than another if it has greater aggregate well-being. This is, in effect, a utilitarian approach to population ethics. The total view says that it's always better to add an extra life, if the life is good enough. It thus supports the longtermist view of existential risks. But it also implies what is known as the Repugnant Conclusion: that you can make the world a better place by doubling the population while making people's lives a little worse, a sequence of "improvements" that ends with an inconceivably vast population whose lives are only just worth living. Sufficient numbers make up for lower average well-being, so long as the level of well-being remains positive.

Many regard the Repugnant Conclusion as a refutation of the total view. MacAskill does not. "In what was an unusual move in philosophy," he reports, "a public statement was recently published, cosigned by twenty-nine philosophers, stating that the fact that a theory of population ethics entails the Repugnant Conclusion shouldn't be a decisive reason to reject that theory. I was one of the cosignatories." But you can't outvote an objection. Imagine the worst life one could live without wishing one had never been born. Now imagine the kind of life you dream of living. For those who embrace the Repugnant Conclusion, a future in which trillions of us colonize planets so as to live the first sort of life is better than a future in which we survive on Earth in modest numbers, achieving the second.

MacAskill has a final argument, drawing on work by Parfit and by economist-philosopher John Broome. "Though the Repugnant Conclusion is unintuitive," he concedes, "it turns out that it follows from three other premises that I would regard as close to indisputable." The details are technical, but the upshot is a paradox: the premises of the argument seem true, but the conclusion does not. As it happens, I am not convinced that the premises are compelling once we distinguish those who exist already from those who may or may not come into existence, as we did with MacAskill's nephew and nieces. But the main thing to say is that basing one's ethical outlook on the conclusion of a paradox is bad form. It's a bit like concluding from the paradox of the heap—adding just one grain of sand is not enough to turn a non-heap into a heap; so, no matter how many grains we add, we can never make a heap of sand—that there are no heaps of sand. This is a far cry from MacAskill's "simple" starting point.

Nor does MacAskill stop here; he goes well beyond the Repugnant Conclusion. Since it's not just human well-being that counts, for him, he is open to the view that human extinction wouldn't be so bad if we were replaced by another intelligent species, or a civilization of conscious AIs. What matters to the longtermist is aggregate well-being, not the survival of humanity.

Nonhuman animals count, too. Though their capacity for well-being varies widely, "we could, as a very rough heuristic, weight animals' interests by the number of neurons they have." When we do this, "we get the conclusion that our overall views should be almost entirely driven by our views on fish." By MacAskill's estimate, we humans have fewer than a billion trillion neurons altogether, whereas wild fish have three billion trillion. In the total view, they matter three times as much as we do.

Don't worry, though. We shouldn't put their lives before our own, since there is reason to believe their lives are terrible. "If we assess the lives of wild animals as being worse than nothing on average, which I think is plausible (though uncertain)," MacAskill writes, "we arrive at the dizzying conclusion that from the perspective of the wild animals themselves, the enormous growth and expansion of *Homo sapiens* has been a good thing." That's because human growth and expansion are sparing them from all that misery. From this perspective, the anoxic oceans of six-degree warming come as a merciful release.

IN PLATO's *Republic*, prospective philosopher-kings begin their education in dialectic or abstract reasoning at age thirty, after years of gymnastics, music, and math. At thirty-five, they are assigned jobs in the administration of the city, like minor civil servants. Only at the age of fifty do they turn to the Good itself, leaving the cave of political life for the sunlight of philosophy, a gift they repay by deigning to rule.

MacAskill is just thirty-five. But like a philosopher-king, he follows the path of dialectic from the shadows of convention to the blazing glare of a new moral vision, returning to the cave to tell us some of what he's learned. MacAskill calls the early Quaker abolitionist Benjamin Lay "a moral entrepreneur: someone who thought deeply about morality, took it very seriously, was utterly willing to act in accordance with his convictions, and was regarded as an eccentric, a weirdo, for that reason." According to MacAskill: "We should aspire to be weirdos like him."

MacAskill styles himself as a moral entrepreneur too. His goal is to build a social movement, to win converts to longtermism. After all, if you want to make the long-term future better, and our values are among the most significant, persistent, contingent determinants of how it will go, there is a longtermist case for working hard to make a lot of us longtermists. For all I know, MacAskill may succeed in this. But as I've argued, the truth of his moral outlook—which rejects neutrality and gives no special weight to human beings—is a lot less clear than the injustice of slavery.

To his credit, MacAskill admits room for doubt, conceding that he may be wrong about the total view in population ethics. But he also has a view about what to do when you're not sure of the moral truth: assign a probability to the truth of each moral view, "then take the action that is the best compromise between those views—the action with the highest expected value." This raises problems of both theory and practice.

In practice, there is a threat that longtermist thinking will dominate expected value calculations in the same way as tiny risks of human extinction. If there is even a 1 percent chance of longtermism being true, and it tells us that reducing existential risks is many orders of magnitude more important than saving lives now, these numbers may swamp the prescriptions of more modest moral visions.

The theoretical problem is that we ought to be uncertain about this way of handling moral uncertainty. What should we do when uncertainty goes all the way down? At some point, we fall back on moral judgment and face what philosophers have called the problem of "moral luck." What we ought to do, whatever our beliefs, is to act in accordance with the moral truth of how to act with those beliefs. There's no way to insure ourselves against moral error—to guarantee that, while we may have made mistakes, at least we acted as we should, given what we believed. For we may be wrong about that, too.

There are profound divisions here, not just about the content our moral obligations but about the nature of morality itself. For MacAskill, morality is a matter of detached, impersonal theorizing about the good. For others, it is a matter of principles by which we could reasonably agree to govern ourselves. For still others, it's an expression of human nature. At the end of his book, MacAskill includes a postscript, titled "Afterwards." It is a fictionalized version of how the future might go well, from the perspective of longtermism. After making plans to colonize space, MacAskill's utopians pause to think about how.

There followed a period of extensive discussion, debate, and trade that became known, simply, as the Reflection. Everyone tried to figure out for themselves what was truly valuable and what an ideal society would look like. Progress was faster than expected. It turned out that moral philosophy was not *intrinsically* hard; it's just that human brains are ill-suited to tackle it. For specially trained AIs, it was child's play.

I think this vision is misguided, and not just because there are serious arguments against space colonization. Moral judgment is one thing; machine learning is another. Whatever is wrong with utilitarians who advocate the murder of a million for a 0.0001 percent reduction in the risk of human extinction, it isn't a lack of computational power. Morality isn't made by us—we can't just decide on the moral truth—but it's made for us: it rests on our common humanity, which AI cannot share.

What We Owe the Future is an instructive, intelligent book. It has a lot to teach us about history and the future, about neglected risks and moral myopia. But a moral arithmetic is only as good as its axioms. I hope readers approach longtermism with the open-mindedness and moral judgment MacAskill wants us to preserve, and that its values are explored without ever being locked in.

CASSANDRA DATA

Sandra Simonds

In 1944,
  the French
Resistance
  came down
from Vercors
  in the mountains
to blow up
  the train tracks
in Valence
  to stop
the Nazis from
  carrying
ammunition to . . .
                My aunt
                  points toward
                    the tracks below
                      I look
                    at the wall
                    and see

my grandfather
leaning against
ziggurats of
indigo graffiti,
smoking a cigarette
with his comrades,
glancing at
the cumulous
clouds. To
not have had
the luxury
to think
"the world
is over,"
but to feel
it instead.

In the whoosh of the metro, a little girl
with purple barrettes in her hair
    sitting across from me says
    "Look lady, there's a dog in my bag.
    Lady, do you see it?
    There's a dog in my bag!"
    She opens the bag.
    And I look.
                At nothing inside.

THE GOD GENE
Christina Drill
(fiction)

AT BRICKELL POINT along the river, Marietta asks me if I believe in the God gene. We're ten minutes from a tower that holds the record for the longest pour of concrete in Florida's history, and I'm looking up at her from a slab of oolitic limestone emerging from the grass. The limestone once connected to the other slabs to make something now called the Miami Circle. It is the only known structure cut into bedrock on the Eastern U.S. coast, and they say there's more of this under all of Miami-Dade, built by the Tequesta natives or even further back, the Mayans. But we are twenty-first-century girls, sitting under buildings that reflect the heat of the sun in a distorted and unnatural way.

"I'm being serious," Marietta says, giggling. She reaches over to receive the joint I'm extending out to her. "Scientists say there is a human gene that makes us believe in God."

Being with Marietta is like—you ever spent time staring at a constellation? It's impossible to tell how far apart each star is from the other because once you start looking at each individual star, you lose focus, and all that translates is a semblance of a shape or person, of this beautiful, amazing coincidence, and that was Marietta, difficult to see, but easy to feel. Very easy to want to be swept up in.

"Like a genetic predisposition to *think* there's a God?"

She hands me back the joint. "You have it?"

I sit up. My back is stiff from falling asleep on the porch last night. We'd drank too much wine the night before and I woke up from a streak of pain and the sun. The last time I'd seen her was on our date six years ago.

"I mean maybe," I say. "It makes more sense than humans making up God out of thin air."

From my perspective, on the grass, Marietta looks like a continuation of the ancient stone sculpted into a statue of legs and hips, a distant wide face with hair blown around it, almost in the sky.

"But say it's actually *in* our genes, to believe in a god," I say, looking away from her. "Isn't that proof there is one? It's like robots know they aren't human." I consider the two skyscrapers in my line of vision. They share a suspended pool deck, which connects between the buildings' thirtieth floors by a moonroof in another perfect circle. Through this, sunlight is funneled onto it. Whether the moonroof that floats in the foreground of passing airplanes is an homage to the sacred circle below us is hard to say. It would be easy to assume it was just a coincidence.

I see waves when a dagger of sun refracts off the left tower and burns my eyes as a helicopter roars above us, lifting through the sky in the direction of Key Biscayne. I feel something in the energy of the ground below us: a discontent, or an anger.

"I wonder if we'll never know," Marietta says, and I *do* wonder if we'll never know.

I wrap my pointer finger and thumb like a claw machine around her ankle, but my fingers don't make it all the way around so two inches of her are free to go. Only she doesn't know her flight time.

"You leave in three hours," I remind her.

She groans and reaches down to pull on my braid, fishtail like her own.

"I'm hungry," she says.

I tell her there's a pizza place. She tells me we should say goodbye to this stone, respectfully.

The air is hot and cottony. Marietta lowers herself to the ground, gets on her back and bends her wrists so her palms are flat against the ancient rock, her core pushing herself into a backbend. I can smell her underarms. She is a yogi these days, and all that. I just rest my forehead on the limestone, hands and hair loose, like I am praying at a mecca.

I can't imagine I have the God gene. I was baptized in a nondenominational church with rose petals instead of holy water, which posed an issue when my mother tried to raise me Catholic. When that didn't work, my father sent me to Hebrew school rock camp, and when that didn't work, they gave up. If I were to have gotten the God gene from anyone, I'd have gotten it from my grandmother, who'd been raised Episcopalian in Jamaica. She only joined the Catholic Church when she moved to Panama, it being the only house of worship she could find.

MARIETTA MAKES audio art that sounds like watercolor. She showed in one gallery and now everyone wants to show her. She called me last week to say she was flying to Florida; might she be able to crash? It's hard to look back and recall what I was thinking before my brain rewired around this weekend.

Things Marietta and I have done together: acid. On it we separated our skin cells into colors, like we were made of M&Ms, and dropped them in Chinet cups. We spent two hours packing for a picnic at a hammock, only for the park to not exist. Had the picnic sitting on the trunk of my coupe on Old Cutler Road instead, under the banyan trees, outside the gate of a historic estate. Saw a black and white movie up in Hollywood, took green tea shots at every bar down the strip. There isn't tea in them. Got so sweaty. And last night, we fell asleep on the porch.

"You have the gene. Only a God gene person would think bedrock is conscious."

"I don't know if I am a God gene person. I don't have a backbone," she insists. "If I have faith, it's because one ancestor forced it on another." To me Marietta's incongruities look easy, natural, but no one can see themselves from the inside out, especially confused people like us. She claims her parents were as confused as mine, with America telling them what they could and couldn't be. We're lucky, she says, we're the embodiment of what has survived.

When we get to the pizzeria, Marietta asks, "Do you believe in anything?"

The pizzeria is run by a tattooed tipo and serves small, soft-dough pies, the kind you eat with a knife and fork between heavy pours of wine. It is the kind of spot that won't last much longer, that will soon be razed for a luxury restaurant group. We split burrata, messy and wet, and a pizza with eggplant instead of cheese.

"I believe that..." I start, then stop. I believe that definitely, things aren't great. Miami is sinking. Communities kicked out of Coconut Grove twenty years ago are now being kicked out of Overtown, where the rich will build tall towers with distant views. That there is no preservation, except to put money behind architectural homages to the people and the land. That it's all revenue. That I am attuned to the franticness in the air, but also to the delirious hope that humanity can be saved, even as it's threatened every day. Not that there aren't breakthroughs, not that there aren't strong movements—this is just what I believe.

"Depress me more, what else," she says softly. She rips a burnt piece of pizza and chews it. "Can you make it sadder for me to leave?"

Back to the Miami Circle. In 1999, when they demolished the building that revealed the ancient bedrock, an archaeologist at UF thought he was looking at was the sink of a septic tank. Its dimensions were almost identical. Why must we keep folding one world into another? I want to yell. It causes death first, and eventually more life, but never the life that was before. Death, I say to depress her, feels real. Not just in the conventional way of *no life*, but in the collapsing. I wonder if it's possible to live between the folding, without dying yourself. This is what I try to express.

"I don't buy it. What are you folding away?"

Drill

I tell her she has so many questions I don't have the answers to.

"By silence," she jokes when I don't say anything, "you mean death?"

I am not sure if I blush, but there is a heat in my chest.

HER FLIGHT is in two hours, so we finish our crust and head out. I picture her pink sarong swirling from my patio chair, one end fraying as it brushed the concrete, dragged by the wind. Now it hangs snug against her hip.

For all the questions I've been asked by her this weekend, she doesn't ask about Jack at all. But I tell her anyway—he is in Baja California, tracking manatees who've eaten poisonous algae that grows on the underbelly of a species of water lettuce; how it's the opposite of friendly symbiosis you learn about in biology. His job is to ensure the manatees don't ingest any more of the lettuce, with as little intervention as possible. That means the manatees still die.

"I'm going to miss your house," Marietta says, "I'm going to miss that seashell molding your painting white. I think you'll miss it too, if you ever leave."

"You wanna say goodbye to it too, respectfully?"

"To what?"

"To my house."

"Oh. I already did," she smirks.

We're off to the airport in my coupe. I love this old 3 Series, even though I can't afford new parts. It needs its bumper fixed from riding so low.

Jack and I chose our house virtually—the landlord did our showing on

FaceTime and we said, looks good. We'd seen the wide wooden entrance, the hardwood floors and thought yes, we love it, it has character. We hadn't seen the rot behind the secondhand washer-dryer from Hialeah, rot that gave entry for hand-sized rats to eat lentils, breed in our broiler. Once the exterminator fixed the rot, once the last trap had been set, once we blasted the place clean, it was a place we could live; charming, and thank God, not a condo. The lease is a strict one year since a developer already has plans to build an office building on the property. I decorate during my free mornings, before I tutor in Brickell to students after school, and it often feels as though my goal is not to express myself, but to distract from the dirty walls, hide the splintered floors, banish my recollection of the rats. I anticipate life going back to normal once Marietta is gone, of my husband returning with photos of the manatees, both of us crying in the bed. But she is still here, and like I said, this trip has reorganized my sense of time. In this simulation, I am operating at a high risk of loss.

THE BACK ROAD to the airport winds around traffic circles and takes you through the fancy Gables dense with iron gates snaked in ivory and other gestures of pomp and privacy. The tops of the banyans on either side of the streets form a canopy that blocks the sun. I roll down the windows to catch the breeze.

"These are invasive species, you know," passing banyan after banyan. I hadn't told her this about the trees the night of our picnic, she was so in love with them, but now I am feeling mean.

"Really?" she sounds upset. "Where are they from?"

FOOTAGE OF BENJAMIN, THE LAST LIVING TASMANIAN TIGER—1935, COLORIZED

Kristin Emanuel

(finalist for the 2022 Boston Review *Annual Poetry Contest)*

i.

one year before dying of exposure
left outside, unprotected
you pace around your enclosure

like a moving watercolor,
heaving sheath of muscle,
hips & hide lilting

as if the world were made
specifically for you
to pass through;

it's easy to forget
you were mothered
into existence—
yes, even the long-gone
once knew tenderness.

ii.

there are still sightings
many years after you
were declared extinct:

telltale flash of your body
slipping over a hillside,
parting grass & air;

where is the pathway you
frequent—the one where
cryptids & myths meet

in their eternal migration?
perhaps stopping
for a moment, swapping

stories & sipping tea.
last of your family,
genus, species.

Emanuel

iii.

we could reconfigure you
through de-extinction,
forcibly extract your essence,
twirl bone & tendon around

your memory like
cotton candy

compacted into realness.

would this be
the first time in history

an animal was ever dragged
from the billowy chapel
of oblivion? all of us

moribund, hoping only
to mother the dead;

dear Benjamin, don't
you want to feel
hunger again?

IT'S A THING

Kenda Mutongi

"YOU NEED to do a police investigation," wrote one of my siblings on our family group chat, "a thorough investigation." On January 17, 2023, someone set fire to my brother Jumba's five-acre sugarcane garden. Three days after the fire incident, my brother received a phone call informing him that thieves had gotten into his compound and broken the cement cover on his borehole and stolen the electric pump.

Jumba's land is in western Kenya, about sixty miles from the village where we grew up. The area, known as the western highland plateau during the colonial period, was occupied by white settlers who confiscated land from the local Nandi people. After independence the land was redistributed to Kenyans but somehow Luyias (my family is Luyia) and Kikuyus ended up buying most of it, further displacing the original Nandi owners. Since the 1970s the Nandi people have intermittently fought these "outsiders" in attempts to reclaim their land; some of the ethnic tensions have resulted in the loss of life.

A few years after Jumba arrived in the United States, about twenty-seven years ago, he decided to buy a six-acre plot in this area. "An investment," he told me. Eventually he fenced in the land and a few years later dug a borehole for water, built a small cottage, and created a beautifully manicured yard and flower garden. He planted sugarcane on the remaining space and sells the cane to the local sugar processing company for about $12,000 every fifteen months. After you subtract the cost of maintaining the land—a caretaker for the cottage and workers who plant and weed and harvest the sugarcane—he takes home about $6,000. This, at least, is what my brother told me when I visited him at his home in the suburbs of Washington, D.C., three days before his sugarcane was burnt to ashes.

Jumba does not really need the income. He makes a good living here as a computer security expert, so his financial and emotional investment in this remote African acreage puzzled me. "That is not much profit given all the headaches you go through to keep up the property," I said to him, thinking that he should sell the land. He didn't get my point, and instead explained to me his reasons for buying the land in the first place: "See, if you don't develop the land, people will think it is empty land and will just take it." He then described how the people in the area are "hostile" and that when he goes to Kenya, he never spends a night in the cottage because he is afraid of being hacked to death by machete-wielding locals. As we talked, I became even more baffled as to why he kept property that was barely profitable and even physically dangerous. I finally just came out and suggested that he would be better off if he sold the land and invested the money here in the United States. But no. Though he might eventually sell the land, for now he liked the idea of owning that property. "It is a thing," he said jokingly. Yes, I thought, a thing—an undeniably genuine attachment to the idea of a homeland.

Jumba was rolling out a perfect circle of chapati dough while I was standing by the cooking stove heating up an oiled cast iron pan. Making chapatis is one of the things we do when we get together. Arguing about who among us did more chores, ran more errands, or generally suffered more hardship while we were growing up in the village is another tradition. Almost inevitably we end up discussing why Africa is poor and why we don't feel comfortable going back to Kenya to live permanently, and why we Africans are just generally screwed. My sixteen-year-old son Stefan, born and raised in middle-class America, listened with an indulgent smile. To him our talk of homeland or African diaspora must seem an amusing fiction.

I flipped a nicely browned chapati, and then turned to Jumba and said, "I think if I were to invest in Kenya, I would go buy one of the dilapidated empty buildings in Central Nairobi and start gentrification in downtown Nairobi." He laughed to my face—"that," he said, "would be very dangerous. You don't want to do that. You will die." According to my brother, there is a fierce network of organized crime controlling property development in Nairobi, and I couldn't possibly survive it. We laughed at my ignorance and shifted our conversation to his recent trip to Thailand. His flight from Nairobi was full of Kenyan tourists traveling to Bangkok, some with their families, some single professional women. I asked Jumba what these people did for a living. "Business," Jumba replied amusedly. I asked what kind of business. Again, he started laughing. "When I asked them, they all just said, *'business'"*—this time he enhanced the word business with two-fingered air quotations. And once again he began schooling my naïveté. "See, Kenda, these are probably some of the businesspeople who would do everything to prevent you from refurbishing that empty building in central Nairobi you are thinking of buying. They own lots of rental property in the suburbs of Nairobi and would immediately see you as competition. They would send someone to set that building on fire as soon as you started fixing it. There is no such a thing as property rights in Kenya," he said. We clapped our hands and laughed even louder.

A few days after we returned from our visit, I told Stefan that his uncle Jumba's sugarcane had been torched. "Mom," he replied, "you jinxed it for him when you told him to sell the land." It made me wonder. Had I? All over Africa migrants to the United States, Europe, and China have been returning to their homes to buy property, either as an investment or to prove to the locals that they have succeeded abroad. Or, like my brother, because they want to maintain a connection to their homelands. Rarely do these property owners spend much time on the land or in the houses since their full-time lives are abroad. Typically they employ a caretaker, usually someone from the local community; they install solar panels and electricity and dig boreholes; they plant cash crops like sugarcane, tea, or coffee—and meanwhile many of their neighbors live in grass-thatched mud huts without running water or electricity, and rarely do they have enough land to plant food crops to feed their families. It is no wonder, to me, that locals resent the owners of these empty compounds or that they gang together to steal or set the property on fire. They are protesting their marginalization within their own communities.

As I was chatting with my son about my uncanny ability to jinx property halfway around the world, my other brother, Ambayi, texted. He, too, lives a comfortable middle-class life as an accountant in Charlotte, North Carolina. Like the rest of us, he had to offer his thoughts. "Jumba," he wrote on our family group chat, "you might consider getting dogs." But this, it turns out, was just another bit of unknowing and unwary advice. "Thieves," according to Jumba, "can always poison dogs." Finally, unable to offer any more tips on crime prevention, we quietly turned to speculating on the nature of the crime. "This must be an inside job," Ambayi texted back, and my other siblings signaled their agreement with thumbs-up emojis.

All the more reason an investigation wouldn't work, as I'd warned in my initial response. "I hate to sound cruel"—but I couldn't help myself, so I went on—"don't these local people have a point. This is a community protest; a single individual is less likely to succeed in any kind of investigation." (This is, of course, what Ambayi had implied when he said the theft and vandalism was an "inside job.") "The people who burnt down the sugarcane and stole the electric pump are angry, united local people who feel that people abroad should not own empty compounds when they themselves could use that land to grow crops." As soon as I had posted this pronouncement on the chat, I felt bad. I was not sympathizing with my brother who had, after all, just shared a video of burning sugarcane and a destroyed pump—crimes he felt so viscerally, so intimately, because they weren't merely attacks upon his property, but attacks upon the very idea of a shared homeland. He was, it seemed, being alienated by his own. The next day Jumba posted a video of seven male workers cutting the sugarcane that had survived the fire and could be send to the factory. "*Leo tutakula vizuri*"—today we shall eat well—one of the workers said, loading up the sugarcane on a truck. "See, Kenda," Jumba wrote to all of us, "in spite of the arsonists' hatred towards me, I still provide the locals with employment." "Aaah, that is an interesting angle," I replied right away. "Yep" he wrote back, "I am not, after all, a snobbish bourgeois who lives abroad"—this he emphasized with several grinning emojis.

It is easy for me to be skeptical. I have made my career analyzing protest groups in Kenya and in other parts of Africa, and I teach about the Africans who burnt white settler crops during the Mau Mau rebellion that helped end colonial rule in Kenya. I am currently researching Kenyan students who burn down their schools as a form of protest. In other words, I teach and write about structural violence, and what happened to my brother's land seemed to me just another instance—albeit with a different cast of characters, and in a different set of circumstances.

At the same time, the fact that the violence is "structural" doesn't mean people aren't hurt. How are those living in the diaspora able to feel connected to their homeland without appearing as little more than colonizers themselves? How can one move away and still hold onto a piece of one's past? It is relatively easy to stay connected in an abstract way, to gather in the kitchen and make perfect round chapatis and discuss the politics and culture of the homeland at a comfortable distance. It is also easy to envision a welcome home absent of the legacies of violence and colonialism where one is greeted warmly as a compatriot and benefactor. But, sadly, nostalgia like this threatens to become speculative—in both senses of the word—even when it involves only a few arable acres. Regardless of the dreams it may inspire, the land itself remains fixed, immovable. It exists outside the realm of longing and emotion, stubbornly rooted in conflict and encumbered by history. It remains a thing.

CAT OF NINE TAILS

Kelly McCorkendale
(fiction)

SHE GRIPS AN EIGHTEEN-INCH length of her tentacle-tail as blood
runs from between her shoulder blades, circles her ribs, and drips
into the dirt, leaving dark muddy pools as she crawls towards a
1994 Saturn coupe, whose radio blasts another Matchbox Twen-
ty song, Rob Thomas's whiny, sound-like-nothing voice further
spoiling the night.

Her back throbs like someone lit a match inside her spinal cord
and flames tunneled straight to her hips. Caking the tentacle-tail in
dirt, she tries to stand but a kick from the left knocks her back down.
She rolls to the right until she's flat on her back. A rock grinds the spot
right where the tentacle-tail once grew from a vertebra in her lower
spine. She winces as her eyes pop open on a beautiful night, the kind
of clear Ozark sky that lays bare both Dippers and Orion's belt—the
perfect alignment of three vibrant stars. A late autumn army of frogs
croaks just beneath the excited chatter of teen boys, who stare at her
bloodthirsty, as if they've hunted down the elusive snipe.

"What kinda fucking freak are ya?" a husky voice calls out.

"Look at that," a twangy voice says. "She don't even have tits."

Her other tentacle-tails, which dance down her spine like a maypole, swaddle her bare torso and chest as she shivers. The feel of their tiny, sharp bristles—rough against her flesh—comfort her.

"Is she even a she?" as smooth voice asks. "Without tits and all?"

All the boys laugh.

"Come on," the husky voice says. "Move those fucking nasty ass things so we can get a look at your non-tits."

"Where did a freak like this even come from?" the twangy voice asks.

"Don't know," the fourth and final tormentor—the calmest, most familiar voice—says.

She blinks at the sky. One so lovely, she had thought only an hour before, hanging out the Saturn's sunroof as the boy with the smooth voice held her hand, when she'd been lulled for a moment to feel like a normal girl.

"We. Asked. You. A. Fuckin'. Question," the husky voice says, kicking a mess of red dirt into her face.

She closes her eyes and retreats into her head, lost.

Fourth Grade

SHE STANDS at a twenty-inch Sony—an ancient wood box with silver side buttons—scrolling for something to watch, pausing for thirty seconds and moving on. They only get five channels because Mom and Dad say cable rots brains. But she can tell they really have no money for it, just like they always buy Best Choice brand instead of Kraft.

Matt, her twin, throws Crayola nubs at her from the black and tan plaid couch that Whiskers the cat scratched up, and tells her to just pick something. Sunday afternoons don't have much promise, and summer ones—post popsicles and sprinkler time when they pretend they've joined the Teenage Mutant Ninja Turtles on some escapade—especially feel like death to them until the Magical World of Disney comes on in the evenings. She lands on Channel Twenty-Seven and pauses. Garry Shandling talks at her so fast with big lips and a spittled voice she doesn't register his words. He's an ugly man, she thinks, features too big for his face mesmerizing her.

Her dad rushes the TV, snatches her up, flips her over his knee right there, and whips her with his belt—a new, stiff dark leather one that feels like hard wood as it breaks in against her flesh. He shouts about her watching dirty shows. Matt holds the Crayola nubs above his head, taking aim at their dad, begging for him to stop.

"Back off, boy," Dad says. "Or you're next."

Mom runs in, asking about the commotion.

"Caitlin's watchin' some show," he says, "about women's breasts." He lets Caitlin crumple to the floor like a wet towel. He locks eyes with Matt, who stays silent, a handful of Crayola nubs in his hand resting on his thigh.

Matt drops the crayons back into their box and closes the lid. The TV's flipped to a commercial for Froot Loops, and Dad clicks it off as he leaves the den. Mom helps Caitlin to her room, where she watches for the hall light to go dark as she lays on her stomach across her bed, listening to the hustle of feet shave carpet.

McCorkendale

CAITLIN SNEAKS into Matt's room and snuggles under his covers. The twins interlock their fingers, like they last did the summer before when they still shared a room and Matt would dangle his arm from the top bunk as they fell asleep hand in hand.

"You OK?" Matt asks. "I didn't know Dad was watchin'."

"Me neither. How long you think?"

"Not long. He thought you was watchin' that show."

"What was that ugly man talkin' about?"

"Don't know," Matt says. "Women's breasts?"

The ceiling fan's steady swish calms Caitlin, as she thinks. "Breasts?" she says. "Like chicken?"

"I guess so."

"Women have them? Where?"

"I don't know."

Caitlin decides she doesn't want breasts if they make men like her dad that angry.

The twins fall asleep holding hands. Caitlin dreams about chickens and the first day of fourth grade when she can wear her new Nike high tops.

Fifth Grade

MOM AND DAD made the twins come with them—to antique row in downtown Springfield. Looking at old stuff people don't want anymore but can't throw out or donate to Goodwill, piled high and stacked on flimsy wood shelves covered in dust. The place smells like decay and the wood floors creak like arthritic bones. Moving around tiny, overfilled booths and up narrow aisles feels like a game of Twister.

Dad pulls Matt off with him to find rusted tools while talking man things. Mom gets lost in rows of pottery that she turns over with care, looking for marks on the bottom about the manufacturer, because, Caitlin guesses, that matters to the plant whose home it might become.

Caitlin wanders back further—the place becoming darker and seedier, like a never-ending cave tunneling to the Earth's core, minus the wonder of ancient, natural stalagmites and stalactites reaching for each other. Dad said antiques were better anyway and she should learn to respect human ingenuity.

Caitlin scouts out old records for the turntable her dad refuses to give up. She asked for a CD player for her birthday, and he said she didn't have any respect for the finer things in life. Mumbled something about how CDs would never be as good as vinyl.

She enters the final room and makes a right into the corner booth. Wooden crates on the floor peek out from under shelves bowed with the weight of rusted hubcaps and horseshoes. She kneels, pulls them out, and gasps. She shuffles through the upright, yellowing paper ephemera: vintage *Playboy*s from the 1970s. It's all women, their breasts out, or their legs open and teasing, as they rock skimpy outfits and pouty mouths. She leans back on her heels and looks around the booth. No one is in sight. She flips through a magazine—then another and another. It's all the same—women beckoning men with their nudity. Breasts and more breasts, and lots

"I can tell," Mr. Snider says. "That's why he and my Jennifer would look good together, going steady."

Catie rolls her eyes. Matt does the same and both stifle laughs.

"Excuse me, Mr. Snider," Catie says.

"Caitlin, we're talking here." Dad puts down his fork.

"No, no. It's fine." Mr. Snider smiles at Catie and chuckles. "What is it Catie?"

"What do you mean by 'developed' and 'tee and aye?'"

"She's well-endowed."

"Well-endowed?" The lone video the girls had to watch the year before on getting their periods referred to everything as "puberty," as in "during puberty your body goes through many changes." Then it talked generally about the monthly cycle and wearing a bra, which Julie Johnson already did. At the end of the video, everyone got a pamphlet with a colorful diagram of the uterus and ovaries. That was it. Sex Ed for girls in the Ozarks.

"Up top."

"Up top?"

"For God's sake, Caitlin," Dad says. "Stop playing dumb."

Mr. Snider laughs. "It's OK Mike. Looks like it's not just her body that's underdeveloped."

Both men chuckle.

"She's got huge breasts," Mr. Snider says. "'Tee and aye' means tits and ass."

"How big?" Dad asks.

"Cs," Mr. Snider says. "Maybe Ds. Takes after her mama." He bites into his chicken fried steak. "And I like that."

Catie puts her fork down. She gives Matt some side-eye, but he's looking straight ahead, confused but laughing. He finally side-eyes Catie and just shrugs.

Seventh Grade

SHE FIRST NOTICES THEM in the bathroom. She jumps out of the shower, and there they are—just staring at her in the mirror with tiny pink, protruding eyes.

Matt is banging on the door for Catie to hurry up because they're going to be late for the first day of seventh grade. But she freezes. These tiny buds have sprouted over night, and they hold her gaze in the mirror's foggy reflection. They aren't baby fat left over from childhood. Since the night of dinner with Mr. Snider a year earlier, she's grown over a foot and slimmed down, becoming almost lanky. Every month, she's lost more and more of her cherub appearance. These fleshy buds must be breasts.

She feels them. The mounds, no more than anthills, soft and doughy. Not much to speak of—not yet—but she's been looking at her mother since the Garry Shandling evening years past when she was nine and become hyperaware of what awaits her. Huge breasts. And voluptuous hips. If genes prevail, she's destined to be a curvy, shapely woman men like Mr. Snider ogle in a *Playboy*. Only the week before she'd seen the bag boy peer down her mother's blouse as she bent over to write a check at Timmon's Market. She doesn't want to be a magazine object men jack off to, or dinner table fodder for men to discuss, or a Garry Shandling TV show ratings getter. Or a lonely bag boy's fantasy. She's learned a lot in the last year sitting with Julie Johnson at lunch and in the local library on

Saturdays reading Harlequin romance novels in secret back corners. Since her dad and Mr. Snider called her dumb and suggested tits and ass not just transformed a girl, but completed her, she knew she had to get wise.

She opens the medicine cabinet and rummages under the sink until she finds the Ace bandages they use to stabilize Matt's sprained ankles after football, or other sports since he now plays them all. She wraps them around her chest and rib cage three or four times, pulling them taut, and fastens them with safety pins. She turns sideways and admires her profile—slim and flat. The minor bumps all but gone.

She starts to unwrap the Ace bandage, thinking it silly to not want breasts, or to be a woman. Julie Johnson's breasts make her popular; even the teachers love her. Then she remembers her father beating her the day of Garry Shandling. Since then, she's hated breasts. She remembers the day of the antique store when she stumbled upon the *Playboys*. Since then, she's hated her body. She hates the shape of it. The look of it. The feel of it—when it's naked, when it's clothed, when it's dry, when it's wet, when other people look at her, when she's alone. She was always too chubby, and now she's too thin. For a long time, she was too short, and now she's becoming too tall—taller than most of the boys in her class at 5'7". And still growing. She wants to stop.

She wraps herself in a towel and opens the door.

"Hold your horses," she says to Matt. "Jesus."

"I don't know what takes you so long in there," he says. "It's not like you're a real girl." He shoves past her.

"I don't know what takes you so long," Catie says. "Julie Johnson isn't gonna notice you. No matter how much of that nasty cologne you put on. You smell like seaweed."

"Boys ain't ever gonna notice you. Ugly loser."

He slams the door. As he's become a popular athlete, Catie thinks, he's turned into a real jerk.

She walks to the kitchen to grab a banana just as her father enters from a night shift.

"Do you really need that?" he says. "You've worked so hard to lose all that baby fat."

Catie walks back to her room, passing Matt on her way. He mutters "loser" under his breath. She does the same.

Eighth Grade

EACH MORNING before school Catie binds her chest to flatten her tiny breasts. She wears baggy shirts to conceal what little shape she has. She prays each night, asking God to take away all her blossoming womanliness. She stops eating, thinking this will prevent fat from collecting on her hips and thighs and halt her transformation into a voluptuous creature. She knows a mature body will bleed, so she wills her period's delay with a lack of food, binding, baggy clothes, and prayer.

It works.

The binding seems to press the breast flesh inward.

One day she jumps out of the shower, and she looks in the mirror. They've disappeared. Her chest has converted from raised, soft, doughy flesh with pale pink nipples to a blank slate. She's overjoyed.

A few days later buds that look like tiny flowers sprout from her spine, trailing from between her shoulder blades to the end of her rib cage. Within a week, the buds mutate into baby tentacle-tails foot in band even after the music stops. And he's that rare bird who's both band nerd and jock. He's the wide receiver on the football team. Cate calls him a double agent.

Matt's the quarterback, and only a sophomore. He says Jared's a good guy and always gives Cate that side-eye look with raised eyebrows when Jared comes up in conversation, which says some truth, in this case not to judge based on appearance. He also says to stay away from Jared, and his other best jock friends—Josh and Dingo.

High school has been easier for Matt. He grew into the epitome of tall, dark, and handsome, with a smooth back and normal spine, not to mention bulging biceps flighty girls swoon about. He's morphed into a Matchbox Twenty kind of guy. Normal and athletic and relatable. Cate listens to Tori Amos and Ani DiFranco. Hell, even Britpop, like Oasis or Blur. That started their fighting again.

Matt got the car for their sixteenth birthday in August for being a star athlete and has to drive her to school. They never agree on what to listen to during the ride. He puts in Matchbox Twenty, and she rolls her eyes, asking for something decent, which upsets him. He eyes her, calling her judgy, and reminds her that he keeps her secret and can out her if he wants. He hates that all his friends now bug him to invite his hot sister to all the afterparties post-football games.

When Cate gave him the side-eye earlier tonight asking for help getting out of the party and then help getting out of the spin the bottle game and then help getting rid of the male attention, he understood. He's understood what's at stake without words since he stumbled upon her wrapping her tentacle-tails in eighth grade not long after they appeared. That's how twins work—understanding without words. But he did not help because he no longer cares.

And so now Cate sinks into the floor as Jared's heavy breathing inches closer to her face by the millisecond while she braces herself against a closet wall, kind of like Ripley in *Alien*. Except she's the extraterrestrial, she thinks, and she's terrified of the human. Maybe the movie had it all wrong. Her tentacle-tails hug her sides. Her hands rub her binding. Everything is smooth and flat, and her slender frame feels like a rigid plank under the bodysuit draped over by a plaid flannel. If Jared touches her, he'll never know. His breath hits her cheek, and he whispers in her ear that she's hot. He puts his hand on her waist and his lips hit her lips, trying to pry them apart with his tongue. It's her first kiss, and it's moister then she thought it would be. She parts her mouth, and they connect their faces with a trail of warm spit as she pulls away from him, his hand sliding up her shirt and her chest. She pushes it down, but she feels wet flood between her legs and the spines on her tentacles spike, pressing into her. She winces.

Jared pulls away. "You OK?"

The closet door swings open. Josh and Dingo shout in unison, "Time's up!" They snatch Jared out by the back of his shirt. Cate relaxes into the floor with relief for a brief moment. She pushes herself up and heads for the bathroom.

She has bled through her binding, just under where her right breast would be, from the overstimulated bristles on her tentacle-tails. She stares at herself in the mirror and tells herself it is time to go.

McCorkendale

Matt grabs her arm as she passes. "Hey, what happened in there?"

"Nothing," she says. "I mean. Not really."

"So something." He glares.

"I didn't wanna come." She starts to crack her knuckles, and Matt's grip tightens. "I gave you the look."

"Dad made me bring you. What was I gonna say?" He shakes his head in that what the fuck way. "You have no friends, and they think it's my fault."

"It's not. I'm sorry."

"We know that. They don't."

They stare, unblinking, for a moment, twin talking with their eyes. His grip loosens, and he drops her arm.

"Look," he says. "I'm sorry too. Just be careful." He looks down at her chest. "You know, I can't always watch your back."

She grabs and squeezes his hand before she goes to leave, ready to walk all the way home, knowing Matt isn't going to take her. She wants to clear her head anyway.

"Wait," Jared says from behind. "Cate, we're going next door to Josh's. He's got his old barn set up like that barn swing out in Oak Grove. Except this one is free. And no rules. Wanna come?"

Cate side-eyes Matt. He's shaking his head no.

"I gotta go home."

"Come on." Jared takes her hand. "How you gettin' there? Matt? I know he ain't gonna go. Julie asked if he was coming." Jared puts his other arm around Matt.

"Really?" Matt says. "She asked about me."

"Swear it."

"I'm walkin'," Cate says. "So Matt can go without me."

"No way," Jared says. "You can't walk. It's like five miles. On back roads. Come for an hour. I'll drive after that. Deal?"

"Just an hour? And straight home? Promise?"

"Promise."

Old mattresses and gymnastic mats line the barn floor. Platforms made of square hay bales have been built up about thirty feet high on either side of the barn in opposite corners that people can jump from, swinging in circles that just miss each other. Hanging from the rafters near both platforms are ropes ending in a loop for a harness.

Jared insists he and Cate go first, so they both climb up a platform. Cate has never moved about the world freely, or taken risks. Jumping from a hay pile, even secured in a "harness," feels not just dangerous, but rebellious, but she gets in. As she holds onto the rope, her ass wedged onto the leather strap acting as a seat, she looks down at the makeshift safety grid lining the floor beneath and wonders if she's ready to die. Jared waves to her from across the barn and shouts something about a countdown. She doesn't wait. Just leaps.

The air rushes her pumping legs as she swings in tiny circles. Her arms hug her sides, feeling her binding squeezing her ribs and tentacle-tails beneath her tank top, beneath her flannel, which she's tucked into her jeans as best as she can. It still billows out from her back, where it's become untucked a little. Matchbox Twenty's "Real World" roars to life on a boombox near the door, blasting over the yells of a dozen half-drunk kids, but a wonderful wind drowns it out. She glides and spins, passing Jared, whose face expresses pure joy every time they meet in the middle when he shouts her name like it's the magic word.

Jared around the waist and slams him so hard into the Saturn that it dents. She clothesline Dingo and chokes him.

With Josh and Matt at her feet, she whips both across the face and chest.

"Cate. Cate. Cate." Matt begs her to stop.

She grasps him by the hair. "Call me Cat," she says. "Didn't you want me to fight crime?" She whispers in his ear as tentacle-tails nip at his face—tiny, razor-sharp teeth now protruding from their arrowheads—leaving a streak of red marks. She uses her ripped out tentacle-tail to bind Matt's hands behind his back and gags him with strips of her Ace bandage. She binds everyone else's hands with their shoelaces and gags them with more of the bandage. When she's done, she throws Josh and Dingo in the backseat of the Saturn, Jared in the driver's seat, and Matt in the passenger seat.

Like her, they wear smears of mud, blood, and dirt. It stains their clothes. It paints their faces. It clumps their hair. It colors their fear as they open their eyes on dawn, overlooking the Little Saint River, which reflects the golden glory of a rising sun behind Cat, who stands naked on the car's hood, her nine remaining tentacle-tails snaking free in the air.

TWO POEMS

Ashley Warner

(finalist for the 2022 Boston Review *Annual Poetry Contest)*

SABRINA PRINCETON

i was good
before the missing
side tooth decayed
and left. when i smile,
i don't smile. i named
my absence, though
second premolar
doesn't sound like

> sabrina princeton.
> she is the city
> coroner and i am
> on her table, tough
> as recalled hard
> candy. before she
> scalpels that life
> sized y into me,
> she lifts my top

lip to make sure
it's me. knowing
i want my death
dust poured into
the mississippi,
she plays water
sounds while
calculating my
insides. i can
hear home.

AFTER THE STORM TOOK THE GATE

that pit bull/boxer
they call bear
got out. bucked
his building
of a body
against that carpet
cleaning van
down the street.
then spackled
himself into
the broken
ground of that
new construction.

i ain't lying.
bear big

as downtown.
his bark the
central bank,
an overdue bill
with felt consequences.
i'm scared of that
dog. i'm scared of you
with all that, *what dog, ain't no dog*
nowhere on this block.
now we running
outside because
i'm finna show you.

he gone. turn around,
you gone. it's happening
again. everything
outside me
get to switching
channels. brown black
carbon black
black cat black
pitch
midnight
blackity
       hole
       bear.

Warner

AN ISLAND WITHOUT SEA

Swati Prasad

(finalist for the 2022 Boston Review *Aura Estrada Short Story Contest)*

BECAUSE IT WAS surrounded by a sea of endless trees, we called the village the island. Instead of bowing into walkable trails, our thickets rose in insurmountable waves. On a crisp day in spring, the tangle of leaves and branches was so thick that a young child beached at the wood's edge was discovered dead only after we'd had our morning tea.

She wasn't one of ours. At least, we didn't recognize her, and this brought fear shivering into our hearts. Umma, who stitched our children's school clothes, identified the dead's torn dress as her work, a years-old creation, horribly out of style. But Gunjun, whose livestock shed was clean and well-insulated and therefore the likeliest hideout for a little stowaway, hadn't noticed any unusually bipedal rustlings. The child seemed to have appeared from nowhere only to die on our shores.

There was talk of starting a police investigation. Of course, we didn't have police, only two firehouses. We were idyllic in our isolation, each of us taking care of the all as our founders had intended.

Occasionally when we sensed the presence of a beast prowling the wooded dark flanking our homes, several of us would be selected through lottery to patrol the perimeter with lanterns, beating tins with brooms to scare away what lurked. But never had we seen an investigation sprout so proudly at our feet. We had no protocol to follow, no law enforcement to turn to or detectives to hire, and so we followed our translucent hunch: surely the children must know something.

THE YOUNGEST AND OLDEST seemed nearly bored by the sudden appearance of the child, but those caught in the middle wailed and hid their faces in their mothers' skirts. Perhaps it was the image of her rigid body so like theirs in size that upset them.

We have a special ceremony for our lost children, for the innocent, though it does sharpen the pain of loss and we'd stop altogether if it wasn't a founding tradition. We bury them where the woods come in to meet us, a widow's peak at the top of our island, an inlet of trees boasting clusters of blazing white leaves in spring. The children point at them, whispering flowers, but we know them as markers for the consecrated burial ground of souls lost too young. Death's little kisses, we call the floating leaves. But for this child who was not ours we merely dug a hole in the ground while our children recited rhymes in their classrooms, unaware. Staring into the unceremonious dirt, a spoiled plum of a memory fell into our hands, a round bruised little thing: the last time we'd buried a child. Hattie's and Seok's little boy, not too long after Hattie herself.

Prasad

Hattie had some trouble breathing in her last months of pregnancy and died in childbirth. Seok lost his mind when he lost his wife, took to drinking and forgot to name the baby. He must've forgotten other things too, since the boy shortly followed his mother out the door.

The older of Hattie and Seok's children had taken to calling the younger *baby brother* while Seok grieved his wife, and so when it was time Paulie, who carved the headstones, chiseled out "Baby Brother" and the single year the boy's life had joined his. Seok had begged the man to list it twice, once for birth and once for death, but Paulie maintained that if he was in the business of doling out vouchers for grief, he'd be out of business very soon.

And so the little grave was marked just once and planted with the body in the ground out in the grove of death's little kisses. The funeral was mostly amber light filtering through the high feathered branches, the stillest blue skies punctuated with a single curdled puff of gray threatening to wring itself dry on us. We had held hands and bowed our heads over his buried life and prayed. With our eyes closed we felt the first few beads on our bent necks, warm as spit and just as surprising.

We yanked our heads up mid-prayer, and the world seemed more water than air, thick with the smell of washed earth, clay made clean. Our funeral dresses all soaked through. Umma wore a doily of a pillbox hat and complained that it had done nothing to save her. We remember running back to our porches, holding our black linens above the mud, the surprise of relief—the skies had been so unusually still, we'd known something was coming.

We spared our children the sorrowful spectacle for this dead child. Despite our discreet burial they remained mournful, so we remained vigilant. If they would not forget her, neither would we.

We wanted answers urgently, but we had to be patient with the children. First, we explained death: a sweet man did you a favor that looked a bit ugly, but then you got to move to an even more perfect island, where there were always rainbows shimmering in the slanting light and clouds appeared only when the sun had just begun to freckle your skin. The children took rather too well to that idea, looking around wildly for a path to heaven, and so we had to invoke death's fear. *Never to come back*, the dead were, and some who died went away somewhere terrible, filled with tentacled monsters and the stench of stale potpourri, and though it was impossible to know who would wind up in this terror, the children who told their adults everything they knew were certainly spared. With this the children were rather inconsolable, so we softened the horror: several long-lashed goblins nibbled at your toes while you suffered a not-quite melty grilled cheese, hopped on your unmade bed while you tried unsuccessfully to nap.

Still, those middle children would not admit to knowing the mysterious child, or even to not knowing. They would simply look at each other, tongues sticking out with the effort of the lie, hands in pockets as if holding the truth in their tiny fists. When we questioned them one by one, we could get them almost to break, but then they'd look up at the back right corner of the ceiling, blow out a great puff of air, cross their arms, and, ever so pointedly, shrug. Every one of them.

Prasad

We worried.

Several of us took our progeny aside, believing our own parent-child relationship to transcend the others', and spoke with our children plainly, logically: It was a matter of island safety, the safety of all the children. No one would get in trouble, we simply needed to know. When that failed, we cooed and coaxed with promises of date puddings and extra recess, staying up past bedtime to chat up the adults while we sipped too much wine and slicked off the day before bed. We believed ourselves close to cracking some of the younger ones, but they held firm, the whole troupe of them. We respected their commitment.

ISLAND. Who had come up with that? We guessed one of those first children, one of the founders', our own generation's most ancient mothers and fathers who remembered the outside world, maybe missed the sight of a sky vivid with pollution lying endlessly flat against the ocean. For us, *island* was *home* first, signaling *water* and *beaches* and *beaching* only as a footnote in a textbook.

Ages ago, centuries or decades (no one bothered with the math), the founders, our grandparents, lost their daycare-aged children to a fire. That was all they had in common. Some had known one another's names, had waved in carpool lanes. Maybe one or two had even scheduled playdates. For the most part, though, they were strangers stitched together by grief. Or maybe it was a shooting? Surely we'd heard the incidents discussed by our adults when we were children, but facts had a way of falling from our heads unused.

The founders bought this land themselves. They could afford such a thing, college funds and mattress money accumulating for nothing without their babies, capital from several lawsuits, against, let's say, the party responsible for the mechanical failure that started the fire or the leaves on the ground in the yard for kindling or the volunteer firefighters simply for coming back empty handed, or if it was a shooting after all, perhaps the police for not following their emergency procedures or the gun lobbyist organization settling for peace and quiet, law and order.

The founders hadn't expected to stay for much longer than a few years. Just until they were brave enough to go back into the world. Afterward, they'd come back to the island to summer together, maybe, and remember fondly the grief they'd tucked neatly away. They hadn't planned on having more children either. How could they possibly care for new ones, love them wholly and allow them to run reckless down grassy knolls, knowing how suddenly they could simply step sideways into the morbid air and vanish?

But that had been the point of the whole endeavor: to forget, to heal, to escape the world. And it must have worked, because suddenly they began to, all of them, dream of babies. The insistent softness of vellum fists clasped around thumbs, the powdery smell of soft skulls beneath swirled hair, the stupid chubby looks when they smeared their first fistfuls of chocolate frosting into their nubby first tooths. They dreamt of the cooing noises their first-borns had made when it was raining, the color of the darkened windowpanes as they stared out at the world together, safe, glowing in one another's warmth.

Prasad

The dream babies led to real ones, in successive waves, one or two by accident and several on the first try, so many of them born within months of each other, a new batch baking each season. The older siblings, born in that old world of highways lit by successive taxis and overpasses that looked like arcs of energy crackling with impending doom, were given small pumpkins to care for and shown how, with love, they could swell just like a mommy's belly.

In a family way, all of them like that, it hardly made sense to leave, and their children grew up scampering through some fields they'd cleared, and those children had children, and here we are now, happy as clams sauteed in butter, as our grandmothers once said, though we're not sure if creatures of the sea appreciate being eaten. The creatures of land certainly do not.

SOON AFTER the sourceless child's secret burial, the children began an interrogation of their own on the history of the island, eyes hard and illegible. We hurried on their coats and pushed them back into the big room where schoolteacher Ongel told them what we'd gleaned:

We had all arrived on the island together, equal, immigrants. We had each chosen how we would spend our time and feed our families. The founding woman who had shamed the original offenders into shelling out blood money kept on at what she did, helping us sort our arguments when they happened in exchange for daily bread and fruit and lamb. We think a founder or two may have been librarians, since we have stores and stores of books that we wave toward when the children say they are bored and that we sometimes retrieve to help us reach higher shelves or knock beehives off trees. We think they must have taken other jobs, because no one has written anything down about our island or any of its founders, if librarians are even responsible for such a thing. We're not sure, as we have no librarians to consult. Two of the founders had been doctors, but neither had brought much in the way of medical equipment, and of their children only one had become a midwife—the remaining of that litter preferred tangible tasks like basket weaving and woodcutting to the reading of thick books the rest of us only ignored. The founder who had groomed great globs of money and chased bear markets in the other world felt she could not in good conscience keep up the practice here. It's not our way, she said, and seemed proud when she said it, proud of herself and our island. She tended to the animals instead. Come to think of it, she may have been Gunjun's great grandmother, but there's no way to truly know. Maybe it's odd that we keep no family trees or accountability, but we like it that way, all of us feeling like cousins, our blood mixing like primordial soup.

Ongel parroted our age-old curriculum, history lessons beginning and ending with a melody one of the older first children had devised: *If you can't recall the past, it can't be called upon to hurt you; history forgotten is history overcome.* Our own children were the first to point out, *that doesn't rhyme,* and Ongel reminded them that it was composed by a schoolchild after all, one their own age, and repeated what our mothers told us—history was what was wrong with that old outside world. Groups of people did terrible things to other groups of people, couldn't forgive themselves, wouldn't admit

Prasad

to any wrongdoing at all. And the people they did these things to, people whose anger conceived inside of them with every denial—what right did anyone have to ask their forgiveness? Our children, every color the cows came in, asked, *not people like us?* Ongel mollified. *Who could do anything to children like you?*

But the children pressed on, started to ask about leaving the island. How, we laughed, and why? They asked if someone, a child even, might come from beyond the trees. And we kept our voices light, *how and why, how and why,* as if dismissing the questions and not choking them down.

WE WERE NEVER FORBIDDEN from leaving the island, we simply hadn't bothered to hack through nature's thorny fence. We were safer here, together. Our air was purer, even if the mosquito count was higher. The founders had bought a remote plot astonishingly larger than the area cleared to live on. When they'd put the finishing touches on their utopia, they reseeded their tracks out, obscuring any path from that old world to our island. They barred intruders but encouraged their children to revisit the world with mildly mustered enthusiasm. They asked their oldest boy on his fifteenth birthday if he would want to be sent to a boarding school, back out in that other world, but his memories of it were hazed with his parents' grief, with gunfire or ordinary fire, who knew.

So the boy stayed. The couple who baked sourdough breads and more indulgent things had just had a third child, and the woman had gotten a case of the post-blues, and the oldest of our island's brood found himself with his first job. With all those bright new babies and swelled bellies bumping around the place, the business would be bursting with birthday orders.

The blue woman was tickled pink as she witnessed the island's true draw on its oldest boy: each afternoon after the ovens emptied, he swept flour from the floor with an eye to the window, and each afternoon after the island's oldest girl grazed her goats, she brought them home the long way through the market, dawdling in the square. He would ask the bakers if he could have the last bun and wrap it lovingly with twine to bring out to the girl whose pleased laughter sounded like the bells her goats wore on their ankles. The bakers began shaping their buns into hearts, studded with chocolate and smothered in strawberries, and though these buns nearly sold out each day and were directly responsible for a late wave of babies, they made sure there was always one remaining to stoke the children's fledging romance. The boy wasn't imaginative enough to fathom the reason behind this change in recipe, and the girl couldn't resist noticing. The bells grew louder and lovelier.

Some nights when the island gathered around a great big fire to celebrate the coming or going of warm weather, the two oldest children would sit just akimbo to the group, a stone's throw away but also a yell. Whatever they whispered evaporated into the mist of chirping crickets and the young ones chasing each other in dizzying patterns. Their murmuring delighted the founders, who had been so jaded by grief and then so consumed by their bright new babies that for a time they had forgotten the giddy rush of proposals. They discussed whether it was their duty to guide the boy, who was barely able to sound out a word as long as "engagement" when they plucked him from the old world, or to keep quiet and let things develop, and as they passed this question around the fire again and again for years, the boy instinctively fashioned a tiny ring of sourdough to signal his feelings, and so the founders simply had to tell him what he'd meant by this gesture and what it ought to mean to the girl. The young couple rushed headlong into marriage and served chocolate-studded strawberry-smothered buns at the island's first wedding, and the outside world receded further.

These days our island's first sweet couple—that's how we thought of them, a collective first kiss—barely clung to life, but they were alive still, with us. They didn't do much in the way of advice, but they babbled to each other adoringly and this comforted us a great deal in these times of torment and confusion.

AS SUMMER WARMED we discovered we could sweat the obstinacy from our children to obtain answers. The more social parents among us organized a complicated round-robin soccer schedule, and the rest, whose jobs or multitudes of offspring wouldn't allow for extracurricular involvement, ordered their children to run laps around the perimeters of their houses, sprints up and down the stairs. We didn't let them open their windows or turn on their fans in the soupy heat of night. Slowly, they melted, though still, all we got was condensation: three names.

Moony, Binta, Nomi. Three little girls, with dark hair in braids down their backs, tied with black ribbons. None were soccer camp girls.

We tried Moony first and realized how she had earned the nickname. She flapped her butterfly lashes at us, seeming not to remember the dead child in question, and burst into song if we pressed her too hard. Nursery rhymes, mostly, though also a dirty limerick that made several of us blush. Binta, an intelligent-seeming girl who we were sure was the brains behind the whole thing, began to bite as if she were a rabid dog, and then suddenly clung to our legs wailing until Gunjun returned from grazing the goats and snatched her child home, shouting at us we'd gone too far. Nomi, beloved on our island for her chirp, was a perpetual ringleader, bossypants, know-it-all. Ongel adored her. We counted on her to kiss our parental asses with answers.

But she wasn't too interested. The one time we could find her by herself, unaccompanied by adult chaperone or fellow intern of mischief, she sat quite still in her backyard, perched on the tire she'd cut from the swing we'd installed. All the children had them, identical, wrangled from the rusted jeeps that lay unnecessary and unused in the abandoned lot past the farming fields. She was staring up at the tree it had once hung from. She blinked at it a few times, shrugged. *The trees drowned her*, she said, and the more we insisted, the more she did, too. Finally she wrapped her arms around herself and muttered only, *Ask Verdelle*.

Where is she, we asked, and she shrugged. *Where she always is.*

Prasad

WE COULDN'T QUITE picture her in our heads, Verdelle. A young girl in a uniform with a braid down her back like the rest. That much was easy. Harder was plucking her from the mass of schoolchildren. We had an impression of her fingers pressed against the glassmaker's window, but not the furrowed intensity of her unblinking eyes. The precocity of her special basket for running errands, but not the hypnotic quality of her crisply adult voice.

The girl finally crystalized in our minds when we could recall her brother: Hattie's boy, born early and wriggly. Verdelle, her father's dutiful nurse, *baby brother*'s avid champion. Her little arms pumping as she hustled to the store for diapers when Seok couldn't bear the pity of the town. Placing a custom order for a beautiful glass rattle the mottled amber-honey color of sunshine after saving up some coins she'd earned or found. When the boy died she'd gone mute, Ongel remembered. Stopped answering questions, didn't seem to soak up the lessons skittering across the blackboard. She would read thick textbooks from the island backstock no one bothered with, or else stare out her window at the grove of white leaves.

If only we could remember how the funeral went. Whether we completed the ceremonies or simply fled in the rain, whether the words *lord save those left behind* fell from our mouths into the wet earth unused, whether little Verdelle's face had gone from cherry to stone at our heartlessness—who's to say.

We found her at the widow's peak of our lost children, sitting on a carpet of death's scattered little kisses. Verdelle looked struck when we relayed Nomi's theory for the mysterious child. *She told you? Just like that?* We shook our heads dumbly: *She only said it was the trees.* Verdelle wore an expression of smug assurance, looked like she might settle into a long period of silence like the rest of them.

But we didn't have patience for that any longer and didn't have to think too hard about bullying the girl. Her father was reliably drunk after all, asleep as often as he was bumbling to himself at headstone-carver Paulie's place, who also brewed and sold his own liquor. Some say it's a miracle our island has sustained so long, and many attribute that miracle to Paulie's stuff, a vile cloudy grey syrup that a sane person wouldn't sip casually but the bereft could take by the dram and suddenly wake to find the lonesome night of grief had passed unnoticed, the mourner thinking of nothing in the morning but his own head's pounding.

So we twisted her arm, in a manner of speaking, and actually. Finally sound escaped her gritted teeth: *How can I articulate everything you've ignored?*

Articulate? Ongel hadn't taught her that word. But wasn't that why they'd come here, our founders? To tend their brood gently, to shield them from outside dangers, to give them the space and the leaves and the sky needed to grow in a way unthinkable in that other world. And hadn't they been mini-moguls, our founders, a world-renowned blogger who had reported on human rights outrages in big-city nail salons and the doctors who'd concocted exacting herbal supplements that helped us conceive and unconceive before the dreams visited and the legal powerhouse who'd won us the capital that bought us our land. We felt ourselves the keepers of an especially pure lot, untouched by the frailty and injustice of that old world. But our hand-me-down values grew vaguer each time they were handed down. Why shouldn't we let our homegrown genius lend them new shape? We looked at her, our worldbeater, and tears glassed our eyes.

Seeing our awestruck faces, Verdelle almost laughed. *Have you heard of asthma?* She looked at us expectantly, and it was our turn to plead ignorance. *Malaria? Pre-eclampsia? Pulmonary embolisms?* When our fish mouths stayed open she sighed at our stupidity. She patted the ground beside her and said *lay with me*, and so we did.

Maybe only some of us wondered how strange we looked, adults splayed like a garden of starfish. Overhead, branches crowded the sky's clouded face gazing at us, unimpressed as Verdelle's. Grass tickled our necks. Crickets announced themselves. Small creatures rooted for and hid their suppers in the underbrush so close to our prone scalps. Wind skimmed our skin and when we closed our eyes the sun showed us rosy patterns.

We'd forgotten why we'd surrendered ourselves to earth when we heard Verdelle's voice again, nearly lost to the small comforting noises of the simple life all around us.

You left him there. All alone, without Mama. And then she erupted, lungs gasping for air between snotty sobs: the trees, she explained finally in terms we could understand, the trees that had taken her little brother had taken the girl in question, too, and hadn't we known all along, and wasn't it time we did something? *Protect us.* Her pleading voice rough and cracked like bark. We tried to pet and reassure her, but she spat at us, *you buncha little bitches*, and one of us may have slapped her for that, but then we sobered and recollected ourselves.

Dig up the bodies, she said.

WE WAITED for the late afternoon, for the heat to drip from the air. We dug up the bodies, dirt collecting under our nails and in our shoes and somehow behind our ears like perfume. She'd furled a practice book into a megaphone and barked the orders while kernels of ache nestled into our shoulders and the fleshy parts of our lower backs.

We lined up the bodies, too many, in rows. Arranging them chronologically was impossible, we'd forgotten which bodies belonged to which headstones, and each of them looked impossibly fleshed, like they'd been lost just yesterday. We lined them up by size, from bread loaf to fawn. Tired looks on their faces, as if long-lashed goblins had woken them from their naps.

All of them?

She put the megaphone down. Gave one sharp nod.

We drew scalpels in lines from sternums to navels, and each time we found a crumple of crusted leaves suffocating their tiny lungs.

THE GIRL WAS KIND to us when we repented, but firm. We could wait for your father, we suggested, and her laughter was cold. Of the several reasons to delay, even we knew most were based in cowardice.

She rallied us.

We sharpened our farming utensils, siphoned gasoline from the rusted-out Wranglers in a forgotten heap taken over by creeping vines and animals burrowing for homes. As the sun went down, we gathered what we could burn, and with torches belching orange flames we marched into the woods to face down the dark, the trees that were our gods, our historians and our keepers and our fate. The trees that encircled and kept us.

LITTLE ROCK SQUAWK
OR
PERSEVERANCE AT THE POND

Evaristo Rivera

STANDING IN THE CHILL shallow waters of the pond I begin to hear the sound of a saxophone behind me—at the shoreline. But it isn't your usual or pleasant kind of playing. No structure, just repetition. So, instead, it's the kind that sounds like someone trying to get you to thinking when all you want to do is feel. And, at this point? It's killing me. I don't mind if I'm out here and someone wants to set a mellow tone and I don't mind if I'm in a lounge being pulled to a more pensive place—but as I'm casting out my yellow rooster tail for the fourth hour, having had little luck with the fishes and stewing in my frustration, the last thing I want is someone telling me what to think over, and over, and over, and over. So, I begin to feel upset and I begin to wonder why I let these things get to me and why I feel an urge to snap and turn to let this brass-blowing-bastard know that they need to shut the-fuck up.

But I take a deep breath

think of my own task
I take another deep breath and I think of the player's feelings.
I close my eyes and listen; I think about what they're doing
    and what it must mean to them.
I feel my anger start to fall with every note
and
in the wake of my frustration
my eyes are clear and watery
I think of my inability to help anybody,
                    let alone myself.
I feel the pain of pangs I feel at the thought of my mother's wounds.

I think of dreams I used to have, when I believed that dreams were
everything.

And it's there, with eyes filled, that I begin to understand where
they're trying to get me—or get themselves to.

    Their playing is slow, but with each sudden honk, or dry pressing
of the keys, or something that sounds like dry heaving through the
end of the horn—with each note and note that follows, they're letting
me hear their thoughts in that moment.
    Or maybe they're not even thoughts, maybe they're not even
feelings, just moments of feeling, portions of sadness, anger, love,
compassion clipped and sewn together as they're rapidly drawn from

a well of memories, otherwise unknown to me. Maybe their week's been shit, too, fuck, I don't know. I may not understand them, but isn't it possible that not everything is meant to be completely understood, that some things are only supposed to be felt as feelings, maybe even less than feeling?

When I realize this, when I leave behind what I wanted from this world and instead come to terms with what it is—something entirely too much to know—I remember what it means to be human, to feel alone, and to decide whether you want to embrace that solitude or find others to fill the air.

My wrist is moving, I feel the water 'round my knees.
I've had my eyes closed, but really they're quite open.
I've had my heart closed, but really it's quite open.
I've had my eyes closed as I keep casting and reeling, casting and reeling,
aiming for a fish I don't quite know is there or not.
And then I feel a nibble,
then I slow my hand down a sec, then I speed up,
and repeat, and repeat, and repeat, and jiggle, and repeat,
and repeat, and flick, and repeat, and repeat, and slow and repeat, *then* I feel the bite, *then* I pull, *then* I hold the rod up, set my drag, begin the steady turning of my hand, and the sax—the sax starts shrieking, and it hollers louder as a fat trout flies up from the flat topped water and slaps BIG, back down into the stillness, where only the keen-eyed would see the small ripples 'round my line. With flattened barbs, I have to chase this fish.

Rivera

The sax starts whining high.

        It starts letting out cries and I can feel them in the
        curve of my spine as my rod bends to the whim
        of the fish at the end of the line—as I pull, and
        churn and pull until my arms burn, with brown
        fingers white and pink and
        PAH!. . .

    this time, the line snaps, this time I lose yet another lure—
another fish,

        and this time I turn and look at the sax player
    to give them a subtle smile or a thumbs up in recognition
of the moment we just shared together.

And it's when I turn that I catch them as they squat slightly—
wings cast wide—as they do a little jump and fly off.

And I realize, then, how much a Great Blue Heron can sound
like a sax, and how big of feelings a bird can draw out of a tired
embittered fool like me.

I begin to feel my body rise

        and I can believe

                in what freedom must feel like

                        and the release it would provide.

POST-LITERATURE

Ian Maxton

(fiction)

OUTSIDE THE WIRE, we learned to live—barely, then all at once: hard years in dirt, blockades, lights in the bay and over the mountains. Within the wire, things happened slowly. From here, it looked like a creature deflating, flattening in on itself, the shape growing outward as it lost mass and nearly swallowed us. But it was hollow in the end, and then we were free.

This happened. How and why has been recounted elsewhere, though scholars still argue. For years no tavern or dinner party was free of an argument; people would discuss it with their partners in bed or with strangers in the park. There was no other subject pressing with such force on our minds. In the interregnum—that beginning of history disguised as an end—it seemed that there was nothing more important, no brighter line demarcating oneself from others. There were books and pamphlets and speeches and rallies and fights, but as time passed, no air returned to the husk at our doorstep. It lay inert, drying into dust.

We were consumed by the question: What happened? It would be a long time before we looked out our windows and knew the lights would not return to the bay, would not flash in our mountain passes, that the supply lines would remain lean, but steady, that no one wanted to or could pick up the shattered crown at the collapsed center, and those who lived amid its shards would have to choose what kind of life that would be for themselves.

This is my version of the story, short and flat, but is not the story I am here to tell. I am here to tell a story in the shadow of this story—a colossal shadow. I will illuminate only a corner of it, one that ran parallel to and underneath it, until the shadow began to pass, revealing what was left in its wake. I will tell you about the writers who refused the question being asked of everyone, and instead looked to the question beyond it.

I can only tell this story because I was not one of them, because I was consumed by the question asked of everyone and could not see the question beyond it. A blessing and a curse. They could not look behind them, but, being behind them, I can look ahead. My process of translation is complex, much of what I communicate must be twisted and contorted to fit in the container we once used and called language, called writing. I used to know it better, but I hope my meaning will not be rendered unrecognizable, and that your understanding is still possible. If you are reading this, you are still inside the wire. I will try to show you something of the life that is possible outside of it.

In the growing studies of the Dolōrem Group I have often been incorrectly included as a—tangential and minor, to be sure—"member." This last word is key, because any study that uses it has already fundamentally misunderstood the phenomenon they are seeking to elucidate. Nevertheless, as my name has come up, I must begin by setting the record straight.

I was born in Dolōrem, in the lower city, before the interregnum—never mind how long before. My parents (you should know that even at this late date many of the old forms still held, but that would change) moved shortly thereafter to the Haur'on District. We lived in a community block with a dozen or so other families and I walked half a kilometer to school for the duration of my formal education. After an initial interest in mathematics, I chose a path in literature, eventually becoming a bibliologist. When I volunteered for the labor pool, I was assigned to alternating work days as an assistant librarian, a groundskeeper, and a plumber. Seasonally, I would work as usher and custodian at the theater in the district where I lived. Of the works I will discuss below, I came to know some of those involved in their making—those I came to know at all—in this capacity. It is possible some of these personages passed through the library, but my work was of the office-bound variety. I rarely encountered visitors. In my leisure time, I walked around the city, watched old films, and learned to cook. I wrote occasionally, and did, in my younger years, circle among the Dolōrem Group, taking part in some of their works. But, by then, they were already exceeding my own capacities. Their world was moving forward while mine stood still.

I have learned not to mourn this, because it is only by this stasis that I can chronicle their work. What follows are preliminary notes toward a longer, exhaustive, survey I hope to conduct in my remaining years. The works surveyed below are not "major" works. The Dolōrem Group explicitly rejected such designations, and no attempt has been made on my part to counter that impulse. The complete survey will require further research. I set down below only what I have come to know through personal experience and the first-hand accounts of people I met who were present. These are the works I happen to have come in contact with directly or through very close proxies. This often required what might be called "translation" on my part, and so what you have is an account of accounts, a translation of translations. I am somewhere between the new and old Language. I am among the last in this position. This is my gift to you, from outside the wire, and into it.

FINISHED WORKS

OR, I MIGHT SAY, "completed," "temporally closed," "trapped in the past." None of these convey how these works are situated and how the reader—another and deeper translation hole down which I cannot dive—might experience them. It is best to treat these works as analogous to the novels of the past: written, proofed, and published within the lifetime and under the guidance of their authors (setting aside the caveats and complications of literary production as it was organized in the past). They have a life after that, as all works do, but they have been reserved, chosen to remain in stasis. The work of the Dolōrem Group in this category is collective and anonymous in the sense that many "authors" were involved, the audience itself being a key collaborator, with no single personage having a responsibility to the work outstripping that of any other personage. This is not always the case of the Works in Progress and the Fragments I examine later. These works are, for all intents and purposes, Done. They were authored and executed by the Dolōrem Group in the years during and after the interregnum. You may wonder at my lack of accounting for the specific year, but you must understand that, even if

I wanted to, I could not pinpoint it. Time has changed. And besides this fundamental point, all of these works were conducted across many years, and assigning them an arbitrary number based on their terminus point—the only sensible way to do such a thing—would fail to account for the time in which they elapsed and were read by those like myself who were fortunate enough to do so. These are the first literary works completed outside of what was formerly known as time.

DISSONANCE AND HARMONY

THE NOVEL was originally presented in written fragments published across early pamphlets printed by the Dolōrem Group press. There are conflicting accounts of how many fragments were printed and how many copies of each were distributed. The most extreme account comes from someone close to the project who claimed that there were not multiple fragments or multiple copies, but only one document, passed from hand to hand. This account is a notable outlier. Nevertheless, it is widely believed that there were dozens of fragments, disseminated digitally and independently printed, copied, bootlegged, with resulting changes both intentional and unintentional.

Isolated, the fragments seemed an extreme kind of noise poetry. There were no words, only sounds. There was an unmistakable sonic direction in the work if/when read aloud, but the sense, if any was intended, was inscrutable. It seemed to be a sampling of phonemes across the known languages, with some critics and readers claiming the inclusion of entirely original or imaginary sounds that could not be found in any language. After several years of fragments finding their way into pamphlets and public readings (read always by someone chosen from the audience) the first work in progress reading was held. This consisted of three voices reading different fragments—both those previously published and entirely new ones—simultaneously underneath the Musa Bridge. From outside, all that could be heard was a cacophonous echo, but as the readers passed through—of which I can say I was among the lucky few—the acoustics of the underpass blended the voices into something very much like language, but also not unlike music.

My own impression was that this first performance provided the title, the future publication date, and a brief summary of the work to come. These general principles were mostly agreed upon by those who had read it, but there was disagreement about the order of the title words, the formatting of the date, and, most contentiously, the summary. The readers split into two camps, with one camp claiming the narrative to be something like a traditional hero's journey, an evocation of the Greek epics, but turned inside out, where man controls the fate of the gods, and the last god journeys back to where they came. The second camp, of which I was a partisan, heard, instead, the promise of a polyphonic history, a sprawling anti-humanist narrative stretching across time and following an undying protagonist who guides the reader from the creation of Earth to the beginning of history.

When the final print edition was issued, it comprised six volumes of nearly one thousand pages each, copies of which appeared simultaneously in every library in the city (and on at least a few private shelves, according to secondary sources). Early readers found a nearly endless string of letters and "words"—really, sounds—that in parts resembled the fragments previously published and presented, and even seemed to repeat, with variations, sections of the fragments, as if each copy of the original that deviated (in a minor or major way) had been incorporated into the whole.

Sometime later, a broadside was issued and distributed throughout Dolōrem—pasted on walls, tacked on signboards, flashing on info terminals, left on café tables—informing the reader that the work would be completed on the solstice, and depicting a map of the city with dozens of locations marked. Among these widely distributed broadsides were copies on which the flipside was not blank, but gave instructions to the reader on where and when to "perform" a given section of the work, which they would find provided for them—the excerpt—at the appointed place and time.

When the time arrived, I and a number of companions began to move from point to point, beginning at the Musa Bridge, wandering through the alleys of the lower city, up to the open courts of the Haur'on District, down into the tunnels below the city, and back up again to Memorial Park where, at last, we could go no further from fatigue, despite knowing we had only glimpsed a fraction of the work, which continued without us.

I could hardly describe the work given my incomplete experience, and among my friends and acquaintances spirited debate has continued as to the work's plot, form, genre, the identity of the protagonist (if any), the setting, even the language in which it was understood. We do, at least, agree on the title, which I confirmed with several personages who I know took part in the work, though they took pains to demonstrate why the title was of no importance to the work itself.

I know of no one who completed the circuit and read the whole work, though rumors persist that someone did, a child by all accounts, who I have failed to locate, but who would—no doubt—be able to illuminate much about the work that remains obscured if, in the time that

Maxton

has passed since, they are able to remember it at all, for, by now, they may be even older than I am.

Capital Volumes 1–5

THE DOLŌREM GROUP was among the first, though not the last, to convene a regular reading group of Marx's *Capital* during the interregnum. Unlike the other groups poring over Marx's work—those looking for answers, those trying to match their situation with the one elucidated in Marx's analysis, those looking to prove the old man wrong at last, those wishing to see him vindicated, those who were lost and, not having a taste for religion, settled for something close to it—the Dolōrem Group was seeking not to understand, but to complete Marx's unfinished research project.

The early stages were indistinguishable on the surface from the activity of the other groups: they read the text of the three published volumes, gathered, read the material that may or may not have constituted the fourth volume, and talked about it at length. As they talked, they began to gather notes, to add to and elaborate on each other's observations, and to augment Marx's theorizing with their own. It is unclear whether the participants had, at this early stage, begun to understand the project they were undertaking or whether they were moving intuitively, spurred by events around them, to take up the work and claim it, not as sole owners, but as links in a chain that was nearing an end. Marx had been read as a political economist, political theorist, methodologist, magician, demon, dead-letter, philosopher, and prophet, but, at last, the Dolōrem Group had read him for what he was: a novelist. With this knowledge, they could complete the story he did not live long enough to tell.

Accounts disagree on when the group became conscious of their project, but all agree that the project's life preceded the awareness of it. Soon, notes were gathered, collated, and typed up. Copies were made, amendments made to those copies. They began to intersperse Marx's work with their own, ignoring attribution. As the work progressed, it became impossible to differentiate the parts that had once been attributed to Marx and the parts the group had formulated. But, as they did this, they felt the project suffered from being bound to the page—even as their additions added elements to the work that were necessary, missing from what had come before, what they had begun to refer to as the First Draft—that the page could not capture the energy and honesty study, much as it tried. So, they began to make recordings, spending whole meetings repeating and refining the talking of previous meetings, all the while adding to the story of *Capital*, which they believed would be a comedy, in the end—all the more so for how close tragedy had come: breathing down their necks, just on the other side of the wire.

In the end, the completed Volumes 1-5 of *Capital* comprises written texts and recordings that require interaction and improvisation on the part of the readers that both recreate and expand the study of the Dolōrem Group. It cannot be read alone. It has become a yearly tradition to stage these readings across the city. The earliest of these were performed with some trepidation, some caution, as to whether *Capital* really was complete, was really ended. But with each successive performance, the readers have grown more accustomed to the finished work, and audiences have been known to follow and boost particular study groups for the aesthetic qualities of their performance. This has led to some groups moving to large venues—such as amphitheaters, weather allowing—in order to accommodate the crowds, and there has even been some ironic competition among the most popular groups to see who attracts the largest crowd each year, though no one counts heads. Still, it remains a somber reminder of the World that was, and the readings I have attended or taken part in have been the most moving when in more intimate venues—a house, a workshop, a museum—where the readers repeat the past and close its book so that it may never be opened again.

Cut/Up

THERE WAS A GREAT DEAL of chaos in the interregnum, as vestiges of the old World began to fall away like dead leaves. Some things had persevered even outside the wire, either through necessity, ignorance, or cowardice. Without passing judgement, I can tell you that one result of this was the discovery of a vast collection of books after the death of a man who lived in the city. Few had known him, he had kept to himself, and he had no children (though, at that time, matters of inheritance were much changed, even if they were not in their current state). Anything that could not be expropriated on the grounds of necessary redistribution was left for those of us who lived in the city to sort through. Among these were his aforementioned books—the libraries having already taken the few items that constituted gaps in their collections—all of which were taken by the Dolōrem Group either on the day the man's possessions were given away, or in the following days as they tracked down the few people who had taken books on a whim, asking them to join the project.

Because of the unusual circumstances under which the work began, word quickly spread about the material being used, and rumors began to circulate concerning what the group would make of all of these books. Some even put forward criticism of the group, accusing them of hoarding, even though they held nothing that was not freely accessible to anyone in the city.

Though I know when and where the materials were acquired, I do not know when the preparation of the materials began, how long this process took, or who was involved. But, at some indeterminate point, the books were carefully unbound and each page separated. Then, the Dolōrem Group began composing the novel, by cutting out words and phrases from the scattered pages and pasting them together. The words of Homer were meshed with the language of technical manuals; the poetry of Lorde was combined with the philosophy of Hegel. Diagrams, tables, and illustrations were interposed, like montage, amid the text. Title pages, too, were cut up. And then covers. There is, in the work, a long section that simply pastes together the copyright statements from each book the group used, slowly twisting the language, wringing out the last drops of power from that regime until the litany reads as entirely senseless.

The work was first displayed in an unfinished state, stretching along the walls of the harbor-front train terminal and into the tunnels. As you waited, you could read; as the train brought you up and into the city, the words would rush by in a blur. Each day, you would get a little further until the rush. Over time, the work began to extend further into the tunnels, new panels were added, reaching other stations—words, then blur, sense, then senselessness.

Maxton

Over time, if you commuted enough—and in those days I lived on the train—you began to piece together the whole work, but you also kept going over the same words again and again in the stations you most frequented.

One began to find one's way around the city by where one was in the novel. As the tunnels filled with words, the branching lines of the trains began to represent alternate paths for the novel, and the reader, to take. In fact, in my journeys it became clear that the Work was not the whole sum of the words pasted onto train tunnel walls, but that each discrete trip—no matter how long or short—constituted a work in and of itself: down into the tunnel and back up again. That was a novel. And the next day there would be a different novel, and even if you took the same route every day you could never hope to repeat the same novel twice. You would be standing at a different part of the platform, or the train would come sooner or later than it did before, or you would try to repeat what you had read but you would notice you had skipped a whole line, or not understood something, and then you would get on the train and different words would jump out at you in the rush as they went by, adding to the work you were reading, which was written by everyone and read by everyone.

Eventually, every train tunnel was filled. No room remained for words. There was talk of moving on to the train cars themselves, of even moving out into the city, coating every wall, bringing the map of words to the surface. But if this occurred, I did not see it. As such, the work seems to me "done." Even if, on the occasions when I still ride the train, I find an entirely new work waiting below. That it is there, that I can experience it, these are the marks of its completion.

WORKS IN PROGRESS

I CONSIDER the works that follow—by design or necessity—incomplete. Many such works are likely ongoing, but have not been recognized as such. Still, like the present survey, these are works that can be engaged with on their own merits, even in their incomplete state. They necessitate less definitive statements and more speculation on my part, though they are more substantial than the rumors and errata that constitute the final section of the survey. Limiting myself, again, to those works I can verify either by personal experience, or by the experience of comrades, no doubt leaves an incomplete picture.

It is notable that the Works in Progress given here are less concerned, at this stage, with collective authorship. They may reveal some friction, a frisson, within the Dolōrem Group, or it may be that under the auspices of Works in Progress, the collective is not yet required to bring its full force to bear on the work. With this, we have reached the limit of the judgement I can offer.

Braca's Tunnels

EMILIO BRACA is a writer of novels. Involved almost certainly with many Dolōrem Group projects, I have it on good authority (his own) that he worked on *Cut/Up* and that his work on that novel led to the tunnels project. Spending so much time underground changes one's attitudes about writing. Before working with the Dolōrem Group, Braca was a prolific writer of fiction, and some of his publications even made their way into *Cut/Up*. For a long time, however, his name merged into the collective and his voice joined their chorus. It has, in some ways, emerged again with this current work, which began modestly, as a small excavation in the courtyard near where he lives. He is said to have taken up digging as a distraction from writing, a reprieve, but more and more he began to dig instead of write. Only, this is not a good representation of how he conceives of it. "The tunnels are the novel," he has insisted. Digging, then, is writing. I cannot guess how this work will be read in its completed state. I have seen some schematics of the tunnels as they burrow under the city—intersecting with the city's own myriad tunnels and subterranean passageways—and they do not form any kind of writing, yet, of which I have the facility to read. An acquaintance has suggested that it is the tunnels themselves, the walking in them, that will constitute the work, but I wonder if this is perhaps a false expectation set by *Cut/Up*. Still, Braca digs, and the project must be reaching a mature state, for I have recently heard that the Dolōrem Group has allocated resources to the excavation of new tunnels. It cannot be long before Braca's name recedes once again, and the chorus strikes up an unexpected song.

The Author: Living, Dead

THE AUTHOR went only by Li. Born, like myself, before the interregnum, they were prolific, spending their lifetime constructing what must be the longest novel in any language, though it is rumored to have no language at all. Rumored, I say, because no one read it for as long as the author known as Li was alive. They believed in what they called lifework: a single, continuous novel that springs from the first moments of language to the last. At Li's passing, there were some who anticipated the release of the work, but as it turned out, Li had entrusted the Dolōrem Group to continue the work, stating something to the effect that the death of the author was really the beginning of the work, not the end. There are now two people, aside from Li, who have read the work. These two people will continue the Lifework, under the collective name of Li, until their own demises, at which stage the trustees will double and continue to write as Li. The same operation will be repeated over the generations until, presumably, every living person will be writing the Lifework. Every living person will be Li.

Repetition and Difference

THIS FINAL WORK IN PROGRESS may be the longest ongoing work of the Dolōrem Group, though it may eventually be surpassed by the previous entry. It began as a simple retelling of the oldest story anyone in the group could remember. That story has since been forgotten. The story, though, was told and then passed on to the next teller, who told it in their own style and with their own flourishes before passing it on again. The story has been told hundreds of thousands of times— sometimes by people who did not even know they were a part of the Dolōrem Group—and each time has varied from the last. At one point, someone recognized what they thought was *Don Quixote*, but by the time they heard the tale told again, it was clearly *God's Bits of Wood*. When I heard it told, it took me a long time to recognize it: it was the story of how my parents came to Dolōrem. No one else seemed to know it. I have not heard it since.

Maxton

FRAGMENTS

THERE IS NO EVIDENCE that the following fragments belong to the Dolōrem Group. Though I cannot absolutely verify them, I remain convinced they are the work of the group. All of these I have seen myself.

Fragment 1

FOR AS LONG as I have lived in Dolōrem—that is to say, all my life—there has been, out my window and at irregular intervals, a voice singing a song I recognize, but cannot place. No matter how quickly I run into the alley or courtyard or street, no matter how stealthy I am, no matter how much I crane my neck to peer out toward where the voice seems to originate, I have never seen the singer, and I have never determined the name of the song.

Fragment 2

THIS, I SAW painted on a crumbling outer wall of the city during the interregnum, when I still doubted that the lights in the harbor and beyond the mountains would remain dark:

> A HISTORY OF LANGUAGE: the Word, tongue-travelling, now gaps, silence, leaping mouth-to-mouth, ear-sprung, heart-spread, and, thus, ephemeral—but let it be   captured . . . [Here, the remaining words were effaced by the decay of the wall, which fell away before the words come to a conclusion.]

Fragment 3

BEFORE THE INTERREGNUM, there was a general strike in the city. I will not bore you with the details of what led to this, but one fine day every worker took themselves to the harbor-front. There was not a single one who labored that day, though some preferred to remain at home with their children, or bask in the sun in the park, or walk through the near-abandoned quarters of the city away from the harbor. We did not care to begrudge them for this because, at the harbor, flags were waving, shipments of useless goods were turned into bonfires, songs were sung, there was shouting, we were disorderly. But those for whose benefit we made this display were far out in the harbor. We could see them, and they us, and while we were grateful to have freed ourselves for the day, to have taken it as our own, we did not want that to be enough. One day is not enough. And just as the evening was coming on and it seemed as if we would begin to return to our lives and labors there was, at distinct points spread all throughout the crowd, the beginnings of a chant of some kind. I could not make out the words, but it began to rise: a short phrase, repeated. And even though I could not understand it, I began to mouth the sounds, and then I began to sound them, as the others around me did the same. I repeated the sounds, these new, strange things in my throat, beyond any language I knew. Like this, we faced out into the harbor, and the echo of us stretched across the water and toward the lights.

I do not know, still, quite what I voiced that day, but I know they heard us, out there across the water. I know they heard us, and were afraid.

Maxton

ANGELS OF HISTORY
Andy Battle

I REMEMBER the first time I ever saw a ghost. I was tiptoeing through the remnants of a burnt-out row house in Washington, D.C., in one of the neighborhoods where, in the 1990s, one could still discern the architectural scars from the urban rebellions meant to avenge the assassination of Dr. Martin Luther King, Jr., thirty years before.

As I stepped gingerly over charred beams, scanning the scattered furniture, my eye landed on a toy—a doll, lying relatively unscathed amidst the debris. In an instant I saw the house as it had been, in its unburnt serenity. A family had lived there. Children grew up there. Psyches, fortunes, relationships germinated in this place. Fortunes that were not mine, lives given their shape by the monstrous hammers of class and race in America. The image I saw—the past I made—awakened questions. What happened to these people? Where had they gone? Why were there so many houses like this one, abandoned and empty in a city where so many lacked homes? That was probably the day I decided to become a historian.

Historians live a good deal of their lives in the past. In doing so, one realizes how many ways there are to inhabit it. The past can serve variously as wellspring, shelter, or cage. There are many pasts to live, as well—personal pasts and political pasts, individual and collective ones. Oftentimes we live them all at once.

How can we represent these histories? In those brief moments when state support has released artistic production from the strait-jacket of marketability, one could explore these questions in a robust way on public television channels watched by millions of people. If you had tuned in to the BBC on the evening of March 21, 1974, for example, you would have seen a singular film with a singular name—*Penda's Fen*. "Penda" was Penda of Mercia, the last pagan king in England. A "fen" is a piece of marsh, neither land nor water, a marginal zone resonant in English folklore but largely destroyed by the advent of large-scale agriculture.

The film, set in the West Midlands, emerged from the BBC's Birmingham outpost and aired as part of the network's Play for To-day series, which for a decade and a half served as a kind of studio system for avant-garde drama. It depicts the transformation of a boy growing up in 1970s England who is shaken from the stultifying conservatism of his upbringing by a series of visions that emerge from the landscape, which is alive with a wilder past that strengthens him in his confrontation with capitalism, patriarchy, and nationalism.

Though *Penda's Fen* aired only twice in four decades, its flame was kept by a circle of devotees until digital distribution meant it could be shared more broadly. As interest in the film has grown, two books on Penda's Fen have appeared in the last decade: *The Edge Is Where the Centre*

Is (2015) and *Of Mud and Flame: A Penda's Fen Sourcebook* (2019). While the film is set in a specific time and place, its radical conception of a buried past that remerges at moments of crisis to galvanize the forces of liberation can resonate deeply for those who let it.

THE HERO of *Penda's Fen* is Stephen, a parson's son coming of age amid the Malvern Hills, near Worcester. His village has an odd name: Pinvin. Stephen begins the movie as a horrid prig and a fanatical servant of ideology—family, church, nation. When a local playwright—a cipher for the film's screenwriter, Anglo-Irish dramatist David Rudkin—delivers a searing philippic against the government and the rich at a town meeting, Stephen recoils in horror. "I think he's unnatural," the boy stammers to his bemused parents. The world, for Stephen, presents itself in a series of panicky binaries—wholesome and subversive, dirty and clean, natural and unnatural.

But this is overcompensation. Something is calling to Stephen. He can't resist scrambling down the stairs each morning to greet the hard-bodied milkman. In dreams, he spies a demon perched atop the church tower, which he converts, through "willpower," into an angel and back again. "A Manichaean dream," sighs a disinterested teacher. The next dream delivers a writhing scrum of teenaged rugby players, capped by a vision of a brawny classmate, loins aflame. As Stephen begins to drift away from the customs of his school, all anxious, belligerent masculinity and counterfeit *noblesse oblige*, he earns the sadistic ire of student and teacher alike.

Meanwhile, something is happening in the hills. "The earth beneath your feet feels solid there. It is not," warns Arne, the local playwright. The landscape is alive but contested. On the one hand, the forces of "technocratic death" assemble—an ominous government installation appears in the countryside; a carousing teen is disfigured by an explosion in the fields. On the other, something older stirs. Stephen begins to see ghosts. The revenant of Edward Elgar, Stephen's musical hero, vouchsafes a secret. He pinched the melody for *The Dream of Gerontius*—"the most shattering moment in all of music," in Stephen's rapturous description—not from the screams of angels, but from a whining dog. Scramble your categories, the composer urges. Binaries are illusions. Those who cling to them simply "have no demon for counterpoint."

For Stephen, the past holds the key to escaping a future whose promise is paralysis and death. Clues emerge from the landscape. A careless sign painter misspells "Pinvin" as "Pinfin." It was once "Pendefen," Stephen learns. "Penda's Fen." The old demons, denizens of what the poet Geoffrey Hill called "coiled entrenched England," still inhabit the landscape. Even the Christians were not Christian, Stephen learns, at least not in the mutilated version he has imbibed at school. Penda, Elgar, Joan of Arc, Jesus—through these spirits, Stephen grows within himself an indictment of postcard nationalism as well as the strength to resist it. He remains a romantic, but his assignations with the past are shot through the charge of liberation. He has become a descendant of those who, as André Breton wrote, sought emotions "incapable of expressing themselves in the limitations of the real world; emotions which have no other outlet than responding in desperation to the eternal lure of symbols and myths." He has become a surrealist. The film depicts a battle between two romanticisms, one that serves the present—what Theodor Adorno and Max Horkheimer called "the myth of that which is the case"— and another that serves to explode it.

In *Penda's Fen*, the landscape becomes a vehicle through which the past repeatedly bursts into the present in order to expose and criticize it. In its encounter with a debased present, the old cannot but become something new. Rudkin's method in *Penda's Fen* parallels that of Walter Benjamin in *The Arcades Project*, another excavation of the past in service of the present. Benjamin, inspired by the Surrealists, sought to construct "dialectical images," where "what has been comes together in a flash with the now." The shock of juxtaposition, he believed, might awaken us from the dreary sleep of capitalism and foster a new, politically charged historical consciousness. The significance of the past, in this view, is only ever given by the present. When King Penda appears to Stephen, imploring him to inhabit his role as "our sacred demon of ungovernableness," it is less to fix his gaze on a lifeless past than to puncture the exquisite governability of public-school England.

Like Benjamin, *Penda's Fen* traffics in alternative temporalities, redeeming the dead by enlisting them as comrades. Benjamin decried what he called "homogeneous, empty time"—time as mere unit, a neutral container filling up with one damn thing after another. Marx had pointed out how abstract time—homogeneous, empty, without quality, and thereby measurable and tradeable—was an indispensable corollary of exploitation. This time, Benjamin insisted, belongs to the oppressor; to consent to it means to be asleep. Its ghastly, cynical epitome was Friedrich Nietzsche's idea of the eternal return, where human experience is cast as mere sum, nothing more than the mechanical combination of finite, discrete elements. In Benjamin's eyes, Nietzsche, Charles Baudelaire, and other weary spokespersons of the nineteenth century embodied the exhaustion of the bourgeoisie as the weight of the commodity economy pressed down upon everyday life. Against this "subdividing" spirit of the age, Benjamin stressed rupture, discontinuity, and *Erfahrung*, experience that is not merely endured but assimilated, thereby becoming a motor for change. His dialectical images established a polychronic time—time lent human meaning, time with qualities. Reestablishing control over time becomes a political imperative. During the July Revolution, Benjamin pointed out, militants across Paris fired on the clocks.

Penda's Fen is often read alongside the "folk horror" films of the 1970s, the most famous of which is Robin Hardy's *The Wicker Man* (1973). While it shares a set of themes with those films, *Penda's Fen* is both more formally daring and more directly politicized than its genre cousins. Rudkin was clear: "It's a bloody political piece. I've always thought of myself as a political writer." Elsewhere, he remarked:

> I think capitalism will fail as a relationship of violational exploitation between man and the planet, though I don't know how long this will take or what catastrophes its collapse will encompass. For all that it is a terribly convincing lie, it is comfortingly anti-paradoxical in its profession to have defined, colonised and expunged all contradictions: It demands that people part company with their shadows, whereas I think the function of the poet is to bring the shadow back into the light.

What Enlightenment gives and what it has taken away is at the heart of *Penda's Fen*. Rather than retreat into atavism, though, Stephen marshals the shadows as armor against the irrational values into which he has been schooled, replacing them with queerness as emotional courage and an ethic of care.

By the end of *Penda's Fen*, impurity is no longer a source of anxiety for Stephen. Contradiction has become the motor of his development. In the film's final scene, he is tempted one last time by the forces of order. "I am nothing pure," he retorts. "My race is mixed. My sex is mixed. I am woman and man. Light with darkness. Mixed. Mixed. I am nothing special. Nothing pure. I am mud and flame." As the film closes, Stephen strides off across the landscape. The final lines of Rudkin's script, included as an appendix to *Of Mud and Flame*, read: "Which shall prevail? The Angel, or the Pandemonium; the sickness of power and obedience to power, or the sacred demon of ungovernableness." The latter is Stephen's new title, given him by King Penda. In Hill's *Mercian Hymns* (1971), composed around the same time as *Penda's Fen* and similarly concerned with the telescoping of past into present, the poet writes of Offa, a successor of Penda, that his is "a name to conjure with."

WITH WHOSE NAMES will we conjure today? In the months that followed 2020's rebellions, our landscape seethed with its own demons. On the grand staircase in Brooklyn's Fort Greene Park, I saw a woman tying placards to the trees, each emblazoned with a photo and biography of a Black person lynched by the police. Near the entrance to the park, someone assembled an impromptu memorial to the uprising, spelling out "BLACK LIVES MATTER" with the ashes of a burnt police van. It remained for months as a kind of shrine, replenished by volunteers until one day, I noticed, it was gone. The city needs autonomous public art like this to disappear so that public space may be returned to its role as lubricant for commerce and nothing else. The belligerent policing of the last forty years, and the wrecked lives it has left behind, are part of this project to rub space clean, to make it abstract again, to reclaim it for those who have given themselves to the cult of "the economy." For this reason, the effort to defend Black lives, the struggle for public spaces, both physical and fiscal, and the movement to weaken capitalism are, in the end, indistinguishable.

Here in New York, the space around us is becoming clean once again. The demons slumber, visible only in the mind's eye, only to those who, like Stephen, need to see them. But monuments, visible and invisible, link us to the past. In "Theses on the Philosophy of History," Benjamin wrote of "a secret agreement between past generations and the present one," manifested as images that spring forth at a "moment of danger." These connections are not merely imaginary, since the world we live has been given to us by the struggles of the past. Seeing buried pasts means seeing the future, because in doing so, we learn how to see beyond the catastrophic present. The goal is not to repeat the past, as if that were possible, but to resurrect its spirit, forge our bonds with its protagonists, and redeem their struggles by waging ours. When we pour into the streets to defend the lives of the vulnerable, we join what Marx called the "historical party." We activate what Benjamin called a "retroactive force," whose power is to "call into question every victory, past and present, of the rulers." We redeem our departed comrades by making good on the promise that their struggle was *not for nothing*.

Benjamin, his life cut short by the Holocaust, never visited the United States. Still, the philosophy of history he articulated in the midst of catastrophe resonates in meaningful ways with the Black radical tradition as imagined by writers such as Cedric Robinson and Robin D. G. Kelley, a tradition that has always germinated in the fields and in the streets before it is codified and written down. What they share is an embrace of historical consciousness against capitalism's obligation to erase the past, a series of carefully tended connections with the traditions of the oppressed, a suspicion of what is glibly called "progress," an awareness that prophecy is a political act, and an unembarrassed emphasis on the negative moment—a "total rejection" of an intolerable condition, a revolt that guarantees nothing but liberation, even if that comes as death. Too rigid an emphasis on blueprints and solutions—on guarantees—can concede too much to the oppressor and obscure the way in which the negative moment is also a positive one. Binaries are illusions. Weakening the police strengthens the forces of care.

These wilder pasts are everywhere, if we care to look. When I walk around downtown Manhattan, I see the colonial proletarian underworld conjured by Peter Linebaugh and Marcus Rediker, where Africa met Ireland and crime was resistance. I walk north into another century and see the West Side piers, where Alvin Baltrop,

David Wojnarowicz, and Sylvia Rivera once roamed. These places become coordinates in a spiritual counter-history that sustains what Benjamin called "the tradition of the oppressed." This tradition enters into us when we read Kelley on Alabama communists and Black surrealists, Saidiya Hartman on the Black women rebels "deemed unfit for history," or C. L. R. James on the Maroon chief Makandal and the ceremony at Bois Caïman, the symbolic opening of the Haitian Revolution. Ancient people believed in a *genius loci*, a spirit that animates a particular place. Our job is to conjure a new *genius loci* that splashes itself rudely across the abstract spaces of capitalism. With whose names will we conjure?

When we assemble in the streets, these spirits circulate and enter into us. We are inspired, in the older, richer sense of the word. We are filled with the breath of another; we let the demons in. These spirits are supernatural in the sense that they help us puncture reality, but they are not quite ghosts, nor are they something set apart from us. They are invisible, yet they exert material force in the world. They are composed not only of our relationships with the past, but also of the force of our relationships with one another—what they have been, what they are, and most important, *what they could be.*

CONTRIBUTORS

Andy Battle is a historian, editor, and teacher in New York City.

Junot Díaz teaches writing at MIT. He is the author of the Pulitzer Prize–winning novel *The Brief Wondrous Life of Oscar Wao*.

Christina Drill is a writer living in Chicago. Her fiction can be found or is forthcoming in *Washington Square Review*, *Triangle House Review*, *The Florida Review*, *Hobart*, and elsewhere.

Kristin Emanuel is a PhD student in Poetry & Poetics at Washington University in St. Louis. Her poems and comics have appeared in *Sidereal Magazine*, *Shenandoah*, *The Rupture*, and *The Indianapolis Review*.

Alexis V. Jackson is a poet and professor. Her debut poetry collection is *My Sisters' Country*.

Aris Komporozos-Athanasiou is Associate Professor of Sociology at University College London and author of *Speculative Communities: Living with Uncertainty in a Financialized World.*

Parashar Kulkarni is Assistant Professor of Social Sciences at Yale-NUS College and author of *Cow and Company.*

Ian Maxton is a communist writer and critic. His work has also appeared in *Always Crashing* and *Protean.*

Kelly McCorkendale is a D.C.-based and Missouri-bred writer.

Kenda Mutongi is Professor of History at MIT and author of *Worries of the Heart: Widows, Family, and Community in Kenya.*

Njoku Nonso is a Nigerian Igbo-born poet and essayist.

Swati Prasad has an MFA from Brooklyn College, where she served as an editor of the *Brooklyn Review.* Her fiction has appeared or is forthcoming in *Electric Literature* and *Salt Hill.*

Evaristo Rivera is a writer based in the Central Valley of California.

Amanda Rizkalla is the 2022–23 Hoffman-Halls Emerging Artist Fellow in Fiction at the Wisconsin Institute for Creative Writing.

Abu Bakr Sadiq is a Nigerian poet. He is the winner of the 2022

IGNYTE award for Best Speculative Poetry.

Kieran Setiya is Professor of Philosophy at MIT. His latest book is *Life Is Hard: How Philosophy Can Help Us Find Our Way*.

Sandra Simonds is the author of eight books of poetry and one novel, *Assia*, based on the life of Assia Wevill. She teaches at Bennington College in Vermont.

Ashley Warner is an MFA student at the University of Houston.